PHILOSOPHY

PSYCHOLOGY

PRINCIPLES

PRACTICE

The Four Ps To Your Introspective Transformation

All Images, Diagrams, Symbols & Front Cover
Copyright © by Justin Mark Bauer

First Published © 2021 Justin Mark Bauer

All rights reserved

No part of this publication may be reproduced, stored or transmitted in any form or by any means, electronic, mechanical, photocopying, recording, scanning, or otherwise without written permission from the publisher. It is illegal to copy this book, post it to a website, or distribute it by any other means without permission

ISBN:

978-0-646-84095-6

How This Came to Be

It would become common practice, for when each year was nearing its close, the following promises of starting anew would be made. To break unwanted habits. To get in shape. To find a career I actually found substance in. However, despite this pact, any positive ambitions towards myself would be lost under a sea of overthinking, unsureness and self-doubt. Relationships would end before they even began. Work was just a mundane practice with no seeable prospects. I would constantly say to myself "later" or "tomorrow", at the start of next week", but before I knew it, that next week had become the month, and that month three. Soon the year had come around and I was left without a clue to where it all went. This would all rise to the overwhelming climax of me believing no matter what I did, there was no way out, despising myself for the time and potential I had wasted. Like most people, I had these grand ambitions to see the world, that I had a purpose to fulfil. However, constantly feeling trapped, I had no actual idea of how to get there or to bring it to fruition. What was I missing?

Philosophy has always been regarded for its ability to achieve deeper understanding just by observing things from a higher perspective. For someone who was a profoundly introverted and observant person, this resonated with me deeply. I contemplated studying courses at college, but always found the formal teaching process to be tedious and rigid to explore it any further. It was not until looking inward, that I became interested in understanding why I always seemed to end up at the same outcome as before. Pain.

Regret. Guilt. Wondering 'what-if'? For being someone who would always glance ahead in time to 'what could be', it was time to look close to what was. Ironically, it was closer than I thought I would ever go.

The Day at the Coffee Table

The initial spark of self-examination came through an unexpected discovery while at my grandmother's house. As one of three grandsons, it was my turn to go with my father to visit. Something, which at most times, would feel like a chore. My grandmother to me was the type of person who, while on the surface appearing warm and giving, always had something else deep down to say. She just didn't say it. This made engaging in conversation quite challenging. Despite this, she was an avid oil painter, always offering her instructional books on landscapes and life drawing my way. I never had the patience for it. Having a picture in my mind of what the end result should be, I became frustrated when it wasn't coming together the way I wanted. She was also however, a poet, an aspect of creativity that came natural to me. Being able to write my emotions down acted as a release. An expression of my experiences. Therefore, I understood and related with what my grandmother got out of it. Several of her works were in fact published throughout various international releases, under the title; *100 Poems of the Year*. This I found surprising. They were displayed in the shelving of a three-dimensional revolving square coffee table, a place which was usually reserved for the remains of newspaper articles and magazines.

Looking through the various sections of the table, my gaze was suddenly transfixed by an image that immediately caught my eye. There, between two plain covers of health books, was a bright red rectangular shape contrasted with lines of black text. Having never noticed it before, it was as if my sudden venture of looking inward was drawn to the word *psycho*, filling in the remaining letters. Then, without warning, my hand suddenly outstretched itself, pulling the book from its place on the shelving. I immediately noticed the worn textured cover against the raised lettering. Bringing it to eyeline, I mentally read the words, *PSYCHO-PICTOGRAPHY: THE NEW WAY TO USE THE MIRACLE POWER OF YOUR MIND: Vernon Howard.* This was different, not like any book I had ever seen before. Opening the cover, the aroma of a past existence filled the air. The faded remains of off white had been replaced with what appeared to be a beige brown. In the top left-hand corner in cursive blue writing, read: *This book belongs to Sybil Bauer, 1965.*

Immediately, I parted the pages, delving deep into its contents. Phrases such as *How to Conquer Unwanted Habits, Overcoming Feelings of Helplessness and Recognizing Your True Self vs. Your False Self,* were some of the sections that stood out to me. These were questions that I was asking myself constantly. How can a book from 1965 seem to have relevance to what I am thinking today?

Then, I came to the page that changed everything. There, sealed between the pages of time, was a withered leaf. *"There is a way to break free!"* Then, in underlined pencil, *"Past mistakes need not harm your present life"*, and, *"You can cease all mechanical, daily trips that make you nervous or helpless or frightened".*

"The intelligent person ignores what to do. He concentrates on what to be. We must put first things first. To be clear minded is first."

"This looks interesting", I said to my grandmother.

"That was one of the first books I bought", she replied with a tone of excitement. Something I had not heard in a while.

A hint of hesitation came across me. It was here normally that I would put the book back into its tomb, sealing it away from the light. However, for whatever reason, (perhaps this newfound energy and interest), I asked the fateful words calm and sure.

"Can I take this home?"

"Yes, of course", she replied.

"I'll bring it back", I reassured.

"No, keep it. It will just sit here regardless".

I was taken back by her lack of hesitation. I never knew this side of her. Like the book itself, it had been hidden away from everyone for years. With this entirely new perspective and understanding for what she stood for, I suddenly had this common interest that would bind us together like never before. What followed would set me on a journey to find the utmost true and genuine part of myself that like the book, had been sealed shut in isolation.

The Fateful Epiphany

Shortly after I began reading, the fateful epiphany came to me that I should write a book of my own. One that not only gave clear, direct advice, but worldly perspectives that could immediately be substituted for your current thinking. So many forms of self-help media I had observed provide you with a feeling of "Yes, that makes sense... but now what"? "How do I transfer what I am learning, to my current life situation?" They give you all these points, rules, tips and quick fixes, but forget the real practical solutions to allow you to put these thoughts into action. It is as if they provide you with the answer first, without an understanding of how to get there from where you are. Or, if you are even there in the first place to receive it.

This was something I knew would require a great amount dedication and persistence, but the voice within me reassured that this was the right thing to do. The true pathway to take. For this prospect of external content and internal satisfaction sparked the embers of excitement to a fire that I had thought had all but burned out. So, I started to write. Something I had not attempted in years due to my own insecurities and past experiences. At first, it began simply as a series of illustrations and thoughts of worldly ideas and perspectives, (things that I had always felt but always doubted whether to bring to fruition), but soon it developed into a reflection on experiences as I experienced them. Ultimately, it became a way to actively express my ideas, as well as develop strategies to combat these negative aspects of thinking that effect all of us. Throughout this manuscript, you will be given a subtext of **Four Ps** that will constantly be repeated;

Philosophy: The way you externally perceive the world.

Psychology: The way you think inwardly about yourself.

Principles: A set of truths that provide the foundation for which everything revolves around.

Practices: Putting what you know into action.

Whenever you become stuck in the cyclic structure of mental exhaustion or unsureness, a new piece of information will calm your mind, allow yourself to focus on the task at hand, and abolish any tenancies to overthink and analyse. Each piece of information will provide a release when you need it, for that particular moment. This moment can then be expanded upon with others, acting as a part of a sequence, or ladder, to progress upwards from your past's internal problems, through your current life's external prison, then finally over into a future reality. It has developed into what is now known as *The Four Ps to your Introspective Transformation.*

A **Philosophical** foundation to looking at your current situation.

A **Psychological** perspective to understand why it is you are thinking this way.

Concrete **Principles** that instill a new set of thinking.

Methods of **Practice** to actively keep this thinking alive. To ensure that you do not fall back into your old state of habit.

Simply put, it will provide you the awareness of what you are doing, why is it is you are doing it, and what the effects of these practices are on others, and ultimately, yourself. Upon reading, you will then be able to use the multitude of methods provided (depending upon your current lifestyle) to actively put yourself into action.

I hope, apart from providing some much-needed answers, this book acts as a guide to uncovering your true sense of self. That's right. Guide. Remember, it is you who will ultimately be doing the work. YOU are the horse that is being led to water. YOU choose whether to drink or not. To achieve a total sense of calm and contentment. To focus without focusing. To take things as they are presented to you in that moment. To lose yourself from all thought and feeling.

To just be.

Dedication

This book is dedicated to those, who feel stuck. To those who feel like they are getting nowhere. To those who, whatever they do, always end up with the same outcome and wonder, "where am I going wrong?" To those who are unsure of who they are and what they are meant to be. To those who are worried about where they are and subsequently going. To those who believe there is no way out.

I am here to tell you that there is a way out, a pathway to follow to create and discover your happiness. That's right! YOUR happiness. This is the first basic principle you will learn. YOU are living your own life. YOURS. No one else's but your own. Your happiness comes from within you, not from any external entity or validation from others. So, within the pages of this book, I give you the tools to unearth the true self that has been there all along. To venture forth into following the pathway of perpetual growth. A pathway where a true self of confidence, resilience, assertiveness, passion and honesty walks.

This book was my experience. I hope it becomes the starting point to yours.

J. M. BAUER

Contents

ACT I

Imagine: Prologue — 19

You Must Accept Who You Were: In Order to Become Who You Are Born to Be — 21
- How Did I Get Here? Habitus & Past Experiences
- How to Destroy My Feelings of Guilt?

One Thing Affects Everything: Your Current Situation — 28
- The Hierarchy of Importance

The Cycle of Perception (Why Do People Act Towards Me the Way they Do?) — 33
- Three Sides of The Coin

The Ultimate Principles (How to Break the Cycle) — 35
- How to Forgive Someone (Then Forget)

Different Viewpoints: Branching Out Your Awareness — 40
- One Dimensional: The Power of Editing
- Dealing With A 'Crush'
- Joining Them Together

How to 'Defeat' Addiction — 45
- It All Starts with A Choice
- Software vs. Hardware
- What Things Can I Do to Stop the First?
- The Art of Non-Identification
- Time Is Irrelevant

Life Is a Rollercoaster: A More Active Perspective   53

- Gaining Momentum

- A More Active Perspective

ACT II

In Order to Move on From Where You Have Come From: You Must Know Where It Is You Are Going   60

- What if I have no idea who I want to be or what I want to do?

- How Big Is Your World?

- Your Notion of Success

- A Role Model

- It Is Not How Tall You Stand

- Self-Honesty & Genuine Intention

How to Deal with Rejection   67

- The Equation

- What If I Am Not Given Answers?

- Plenty of Fish in The Sea

Being Alone vs. Feeling Lonely   74

- Origins of the Two

- Boredom & Procrastination

Structured Perspective   79

- House Metaphor

- The Foundation (Conservative)

- The Roof (Liberal)

- The Structure

- Can Peace Exist without Chaos?

How to Be Truly Attractive   89
- What Makes Someone Attractive?
- The Vibe
- Alpha or Beta?
- Changing Your Appearance (Finding your 'style')
- Being In the Moment

Being 'Honestly' Vulnerable   98

Love & Dating Flow   100
- But I Already Know I Am Ready
- What If I Have Been Heartbroken?
- How This Applies to Dating
- Is Dating Even the Right Word?
- Love at First Sight: Soul Mates or A Choice?
- *You Stand*

ACT III

A Shift in Perspective (Intermission)   113

How to Stop Overthinking   115
- Thoughts

How to Make Decisions/Let the Outcome Appear   117
- Abundance
- What to Do When We Feel We Aren't Good Enough?
- Oneness

Be the Better Man/Woman   123
- The Time Is Now
- Detachment
- How to Handle Ageing: The Fear of Getting Older

Did I Do the Right Thing?   129
- The Equation: An Alternate Perspective

The Path of Least Resistance: Synchronicity   134

Meditating: The Art of Proper Breathing   135
- The Breath of a Balloon

Morning Routine   139
- I Have Trouble Falling Asleep at Night?
- The 4-4-4 Method
- Making Your Bed
- Breakfast
- Stretching

Lack of Motivation/Excitement   144
- Getting Comfortable
- Flipping the Script: Using This as Fuel
- The 15-30-15 Method
- Remember your goal

Process of Self-Learning: 150
(A Deeper Look Into Practice Makes Perfect)
- Is All This Necessary?
- Disclaimer: For Teachers

How to Achieve True Focus   155
- Emotional Content
- The Antidote to Fear

Standing Up For Yourself   163
- Letting It Go/Picking Your 'Fights'

Having Sex vs. A Sexual Experience   167

- Are you Truly Aroused?
- The Dynamic: Masculinity & Femineity
- How to Break It
- It Has to Be Earnt
- You Don't Have to 'Love' One Another To Have Sex
- One Night Stand
- What If I Am A Virgin?
- How Do I Get Comfortable?

ACT IV

Networking v. Social Networking   186

- Why Messaging Is Such a Problem?
- How To Text Properly
- What If They Don't Reply?
- Fear Of Talking on The Phone
- Taking This Further: Networking

Physical Health: Mental Awareness to Transform Your Outer Image   195

- Your Ideal Physique: The Three-Dimensional Body
- Factors That Stop Us From Initiating This Change
- Self-Consciousness & Environment
- Lack of Knowledge/Excess (Selecting A Training Philosophy)
- What If I Am Still Not Seeing Results?

Pathways: Job, College, Career   208
- The 9-5 Structure
- A Casual/Part-time Job
- The Perception of Our Path
- Options If You Don't Study
- Two Birds with One Purpose

Budgeting Your Expenses   221
- Some More Things to Consider
- Crafting Your Own Career: Resume & Cover Letter

Belief vs. Faith?   228
- Tripod of Theology
- Desiderata

Saying Things With Conviction   235
- How to Become Fluent at Public Speaking
- How to 'Win' An Argument

Becoming The Person, You Tried Not To Be   246
- You and Your Ego
- How to Come Down from A High Ego?
- Which Is Easier?

When You Reach The Limit   250
- The Cycle of Transformation
- Everything Is Everything

How to Read the Situation (Then Act Accordingly) 257
- Trusting Your Ability

Where to Go From Here? 261
- Disclaimer: Is This Book Ultimately Pointless?

This Only Happens In The Movies (Epilogue) 268
- Leaving My Island

Works Referenced/Bibliography 278

ACT I

Imagine
(Prologue)

You stand before the presence of a tall satin curtain. A warm earthly tone, it keeps you hidden from the light. A voice is heard from the other side. It describes you, acknowledges you for the occupation you dream of, your achievements and skills you have always wanted. It then calls to you to the stage. The light above you turns green. The drapes pull apart. A spotlight focuses in on you. Suddenly, the collective hands of an audience erupt in applause.

Dressed immaculate. Stylish. Hair and facial features complimenting one another, you walk out head held high. Confident. Not cocky. Smooth. Not static. You reach the centre of the stage, shaking the interviewer's hand. Firm yet fluid. Decisive, not demanding. Taking a seat, they greet you with a question. Composed, you respond by talking effortlessly, without stumbling or hesitating. As if all your thoughts immediately flow from your mind without distraction. You are calm, at ease, and charismatically direct the conversation to its highest form.

Picture this scenario vividly in your mind, engrave it into your subconscious. This is your **TRUE SELF**.

Not famous. Not a movie star. Just someone who has all the attributes of their mind, body and soul together in a state of pure harmony and totality.

We are all born with these qualities as human beings. To love, to hate, to decide what of those to act on. Humans who must be, in the moment. However, the moment that is presented to us currently is one of great pain. We get beaten down. Trod on. Made a fool of by our life, and as result we truly believe this is all it has to offer. Unfortunately, the more we continue to accept this philosophy, the more we lose sight of the door that calls for our salvation.

No matter how dire the situation seems to you now, there is a way out. In fact, the way has been there all along! Confidence is something that resides in all of us. Like an ancient tomb, it waits to be discovered by a determined explorer. For some, they are born with it already opened, while for others, their unfortunate origins perhaps have something left to be desired. However, with desire comes divinity. An opportunity for realisation. You already possess everything you need to succeed. All that is required is the way to bring it forward. Notice that 'it' is used. You are a soul encased within this form of flesh we call human beings. Your life revolves around you, and you revolve around it. You are nothing, yet everything simultaneously. This all may sound too philosophical at first. However, I assure you, as you edge deeper into the process of your own introspective transformation, your mind will become more open to the meanings in this book. What you need to realise right now is that the door is just beyond, waiting to be unlocked. It is only your true self is what will get you there!

"That's great", you may ask, "but where do I go from here? How to do I get all the way to there, from where I am now? Where should I start?"

The beginning.

You Must Accept Who You Were: In Order to Become Who You Are Born to Be

As soon as I first sat down to read Vernon Howard's book, there was already a series of questions that I required answers to. Like lingering shadows, they had been ever present in my thoughts, always at the centre of my mind and its overthinking tendencies. I came from this yearning desire to change, yet I still had anchors from my past weighing me down. It was these iron protrusions that needed to be eroded before anything else could take place for this vessel to cast off. How did I get here?

It is not as literal as it sounds. Yes, we all know the talk of the birds and the bees, but what I am referring to relates specifically to the things that got you here, to reading this book. What things have accumulated to you being in this current position? You have been here before, but now that you are seriously questioning it to the point of taking action, you require the deeper knowledge to break through to understanding.

Habitus

Habitus, simply put, is the accumulation of all your attributes that have been conditioned to you since birth, through childhood, and all the way to present day. These include your genetics determining your physical attributes and personality traits, your environmental upbringing contributing to your habits and tastes; and all your thoughts, feelings, fears, desires, relationships, passions and self-image. Hard to believe, but until brought attention to, we ironically aren't aware of the extent these factors of habitual creation play in shaping the early stages of our path in life.

In my case, I was born four months premature (twenty-four weeks), weighing approximately 640 grams, 1.4 pounds or 0.1 stone. As my mother would constantly remind me, it really was miracle that I even managed to be brought into the world without any direct complications. However, this eagerness to be born into the world was a trait that really defined the way I would conduct myself for years to come. Simply put, I would see the end before things even began. Now obviously I don't mean in a psychic sense (although at times it felt like that), rather, I would observe a situation, and immediately conjure up potential outcomes that could occur as a result. So impatient to reach the goal, that I missed the things in between that got me there. On top of this, as a result of being born so early, my frame was one that could have easily resembled a skeleton. People would comment on my legs like it was the first time I had seen them myself. "Woah you have skinny legs". "They are like twigs". "You should really eat something". This naturally caused me to gain a shyness towards social situations, always afraid to share my experiences, and always worried about how my thoughts would be interpreted by to those around me. I was seen only as the shy, quiet one. The 'nice guy' on the outer edge of the group. Never truly part of the conversation.

This provided the foundation for my entire schooling experience from my teenage years, all the way through to graduation. It became inherently apparent to me during my senior years, with my awareness growing to a heightened level of anxiety. Perhaps I was at the point in my development where I was realizing the effect others actions were having, or perhaps I was becoming aware how I was being treated. Either way, the common denominator it seemed, always stemmed back towards my physical attributes.

Aside from school, I would also see similarities in my life at home. Being the middle child of three boys, my family dynamic was one where I was on the outer. When I tried to explain things from my perspective, I would get shutdown, with comments being referred to my prematurity. It felt like no matter what I said, my opinion was not valued. I was in an environment where I had no voice, and when I wanted to be alone, everyone was around, and when I wanted company, no one was to be seen. Now in retrospection, I can see clear similarities of what percentage of me is my mother and father. In what areas I was more feminine and masculine. I definitely can see I accumulated these doubts and emotional tendencies from my mother side, where in my father I saw his physical attributes, and the way he reacted to things. I was brought up on fairy tales, romance and this grand picture of life, but lived-in isolation on a farm away from the bustling reality of the world. Despite being driven to life by this dreamer-esc outlook, I wasn't even remotely aware the effect this had on my position in it. I was always looking beyond to the horizon. Never to where I was on the shore.

You might not think your habitus could contribute so much to your experiences. It's just how it is. You don't second guess it. Only when you get to a point where you have to go back and question your past, do you see the extent of their influence. You have your traits you were born with, physical and mental. You may have been born larger, lighter, taller or shorter. It is irrelevant. Don't let it run your life for you. If you do, they will define the course yours will take, and won't stop until you take action. You have to learn to harness them. Use them to your advantage. No one is born already as their true self. Everyone has skills to learn. Lessons to acquire knowledge from. The cards you have drawn may not be the ones you wanted, but realise that is okay. It is all relative. No matter the deck. There is a state left to be reached. This is to be the first step in your journey. Be honest with yourself. Recognise your traits. Reflect on what others have said about you. Understand that this provides the reasoning behind why you have been going about things up until now. Why your experiences have resulted in the way they have. Rather than seeing them as hinderances, see them as a starting point to go from. Something, if viewed from the right perspective can be used as a mechanism to grow. You can either dwell in them, or make the most of their potential.

Your Past Experiences

The past is a construct of time that, for I'm sure all of you reading, can be extremely difficult to address. It is one that represents the root of everything in your life that has grown to bear the fruit of the present. Pain. Suffering. Regret. Guilt. For me, it was a combination of all these. The regret of past actions. The guilt over the events that followed. The pain of not knowing what came next. The suffering of realizing no matter how hard I tried, things could never be the same. Upon graduating from high-school, I thought things would be different. I hoped a change in environment would provide fresh opportunities and experiences, a position far away from the past. It did not. Whatever action I would take, rejection, loneliness and anxiety would follow. Ironically, opposite to my habitual trait of forward thinking, things would end before they even began. Why was I constantly ending up back at this state?

> *"We cannot continue the same thing and expect different results"- Otto Perez Molina*

As common as this saying is, a mistake we make in processing past pain, is that we anchor all our attention on the events that was, failing to understand that it is in itself the cause to our suffering now. We are blinded by our trauma, to the extent it acts as a facade to the actual truth. Focusing in on the bad, till that is all we can ever receive from it. To evolve out of this, we first need an alternate way of viewing things. First, the degree of severity it played on us, and secondly, the role we played for it to occur. If only we could see that each opportunity provides us with another to reflect on our actions. If only we were aware of the true effect, our habitus has in creating our reactions to certain social contexts. If only we could know that there was a part of ourselves that would have easily been able to deal with this. If only. No. **If** is conditional. If refers to things outside our control. **Only** means limited. You will learn there are no limitations, only limits one limits themselves to in their control. For better or for worse.

Now of course, it is easy for me to say to you; "Get over your pain". "Just forget it", and while in a rudimentary sense it is true, the past, being paved with countless moments of detailed trauma, can still be quite a horrific experience to shift through. Therefore, I am here to reassure you it is okay if you can't right as this moment. This is something that can be done gradually, in increments, and at your own pace. However, if you do decide to take that step, as painful as it will be to do so, it is necessary. Believe me.

All pain is relative in the mind of the individual. Yes, the **context may be different**, with events by comparison more graphic, but the emotional state that pain brings upon is the same (in principle) for all human beings.

Whether you jump in now or in a few days, those parts will be just as impactful then, as if you had addressed them later. It is all a part of the process. You can always refer to these sections in the meantime. (See *Dealing with Rejection, Did I do the Right Thing? & How to Stop Overthinking?*)

How to Destroy Feelings of Guilt

Although I had seemingly been able to manage the initial feelings of anxiety and self-defeating thoughts that plagued me throughout my early adolescence, I still was left with an overbearing sense of being extremely lost. I had so much hope in things changing after school, that when they did not in college, I figured if it didn't work then, why would it work now? What's the point? Fearful of putting myself out there, this perspective led me to find comfort in other areas, in particular through others.

What would happen? Again, I would constantly think about the future. If only I had told her. Why didn't I tell her? Should I have told her? Did I do the right thing? Would things be different? Every time I got a moment alone to process my life, the only thing that came to me were these questions. Time and time again. It was like a disease that no matter the treatment given, would always find its way back to infection. I tried desperately to forget and convince myself that it happened for a reason, but how was I able to move forward with my life when I was constantly weighed down by the anchor that was my past? Staring face to face with the red cover of *Psycho-Pictography*, I immediately opened to the contents page, reading; *How to Break Self-Defeating Habits*. I came to a particular section all about an emotion embedded in my past that had been the fatal cause to most of my problems. Guilt.

"Your freedom lies in not identifying yourself with your past mistake. This means that you presently identify yourself and your mistake as one; you take them as the same thing. You wrongly think that you are your mistake. But you are not. You are not your mistake. Your false-self made that mistake, but you are not your false-self".

Contrary to the common belief, if we harbor all our thoughts and emotions into the pain of past events, we start to lose focus on the event itself, and instead draw our attention to the person at the focal point of it all. You. Yes, these events may involve another person, but ultimately it was the lack of attention to self that caused this sudden guilt to your actions, all stemming back to the tendencies created by your habitus.

I finally understood that any thought that is built on what others might think, be it guilt, pain, or anxiety, can all be attributed to the bad qualities of my false-self. Therefore, all this would not have occurred if I was acting through my true-self. It was like the answer I had needed to hear this entire time. The release from the mental prison that had held me for years on end. I believe this is the first step in starting your journey to your introspective transformation. The art of letting go. Leaving the past behind by addressing directly **what is** within yourself internally, and **what was** externally. Everything concerning others and these experiences was merely a reflection of yourself at that particular moment, a self that was led by an unawareness to our own habitus. So, ask yourself; **How would my genuine self-act in that situation?** (See *Be the Better Man/Woman*). Make peace and accept with who you were, the event that was, and if involving another, the effect it may have had on their own psyche. (See *The Cycle of Perception*). That was then, this is now, and there is only what will become.

One Thing Affects Everything:
Your Current Situation

If you were to break down the multitude of areas that made up your life, you would most likely separate them into one of these categories.

Occupation
Home Life
Family: Kids & Parents
Relationships
Personal Image & Mental Health

Now if you were then to go through each of these in greater detail, it would be easy to highlight what exactly it is you would like to change. Maybe you are sick of your mundane job that lacks passion, or your relationships are fleeting in their existence? Perhaps even your sense of self and personal image lacks conviction; having no confidence in who you are or even what you are supposed to be? Whatever the case, (for some it might be all these things), a question that is often raised is what aspect is more important to address first? Well, that right there is your answer. No? Still don't understand?

Hierarchy of Importance

Let's say you are trying desperately to address your mindset towards your sense of self, but your environment, either at work or home, is causing you to become overwhelmed. It would then be logical to conclude that it is your environment that holds the root to your unhappiness, and therefore should be the first to address. Yes, in most cases a working or living environment (where abuse and pressure are constant), can be extremely detrimental to your mental health. However, although this job may be those things, it still allows you to support yourself in other areas of your life. Without it, you would be worse off. One thing affects the other. It's a pyramid system where each level support one another and if one falls, the entire structure is compromised.

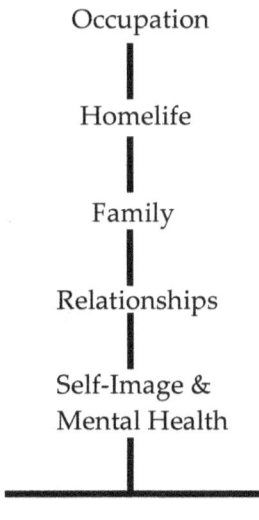

Ironically, it is through the stress gained via this environment that causes you to enforce habits and distractions in order to cope. You may think otherwise, but by indulging in these, you only reinforce the pressures you hold towards your mindset. The same can be said for relationships. Say you have been rejected time and time again. This obviously would have a serious effect on your self-confidence and worth. Naturally, to combat this, you would consume yourself in mechanisms to hold on to whatever pleasure you have left. Only if you were to realise it is this lack of self-awareness and assurance that results in your lack of success. It would then be easy to focus all your attention addressing that, reading every piece of dating advice, or learning how to abolish addiction. It only exacerbates the problem. In this case, it is safe to conclude these things;

1. That each variable/level is relative; meaning there is no hierarchy of importance. One is no more important than the other.

2. In some cases, you will find that in order to address one thing, you have to address the other first.

3. Certain things take time, however by having a strong mindset, you will be able to plant the seeds to nurture the path towards their eventual bloom.

4. Rather than thinking of it as a vertical line of value, consider it as one horizontal plane of relevance, the 'tower' reliant on the strength of all these components together.

Occupation   Home Life   Self-Image/ Mindset   Relationship   Family

This brings us back to the question of what aspect holds the highest priority? See, in asking the question we have simultaneously found the answer. This doesn't mean the mindset is most important, it means it is the one that is most **accessible**. The one that holds the highest priority and has the most influence, is not the one which holds most importance to you, but the one that is most addressable. In other words.

Don't put off what you can do today and/ or think and you shall become.

We have all heard these phrases before, but taking away the passé nature that comes with them, really ask yourself, what task can I do today that works towards my goal? It could be to sending an email inquiring about a job. Research job opportunities or organise a meet up for a colleague. Work on a portfolio for artwork or photography. Do some writing towards a book (what I am doing now). Anything. Asking this question every time you get overwhelmed or lose yourself in the big picture, will calm your mind and allow it to be in the moment. Do you what can today, at this moment. Soon, that moment will turn into a day, which will turn into a week, then a month. "Oh, if only I had started it then, I would have made so much progress." They key is having a clear mind that allows you to take action with ease. Not being concerned with worried thoughts of 'what if'. In regards to thinking and becoming, for some, this may be attuned to certain topics (relationships & sex), while for others, it may be simply to stop overthinking. That is the nature of your mind, and the extent of your task at hand. To unlock a series of doors that are constantly opening and closing.

The Most Common Form of Self-Help

'A cluttered environment reflects a cluttered mind'. This mantra can be found in almost every form of self-help media. It is a prerequisite, a rite of passage for those writing a book to include. Better to get it out of the way now. However, in this cliche come a constant. An immediate action that can be put into place. Clean up out your room, car, fridge, desk, wardrobe, bed, etc. You will surprise yourself with how much materialistic garbage you don't really use, or need. "Waste not. Want not" as they say. By having these external affairs in check, it will be much easier to address your internal ones, and vice versa. By having a better outlook on what is happening internally, you will slowly begin to attract better outcomes to what will happen externally. You should not prioritize one over the other. Do what you can achieve today, on the smallest level, and it will amount to much larger things in the future. Note: All this said, this information may only provide some initial inspiration to you in your journey, and it is highly unlikely that it will be put into motion the first-time round. Having been there myself, it needs more of a relevant context to be applied for. Therefore, this will be expanded upon in the later sections of this book; *Lack of Excitement/Motivation & Flipping the Script*).

The Cycle of Perception
Why Do People Act Towards Me the Way They Do?

As you have picked up this book, you are most likely coming from a place of shyness or anxiety, or have been the subject of bullying. Of course, it is never nice to be on the receiving end of this treatment, as the way someone may treat you only reinforces the overall quality you feel towards yourself. Yet in my experience, half the battle in receiving better treatment is understanding the circumstances which makes them act that way in the first place. As we have all been a part of a schooling environment (or perhaps are at this moment), let's refer to a common scenario that you yourself have probably been on the receiving end of.

You are introverted and shy because you are constantly teased by others. You feel you do not belong to any group, and even when you do, you feel you have no contribution to it at all. All your ideas, thoughts and expressions are shut down and when you are brought into the conversation, it only seems to be as a part of a joke for appeasing others.

I can tell you from experience, these were exactly the feelings that went through my mind for most of my early life. As discussed in the opening chapter on habitus, my tiny figure naturally led people to see me as the little shy one. Too nice to stand up for himself. Happy to let those walk over him. Whenever I did attempt to showcase any intent to be more confident, I was immediately shut down. It was as if, no matter which path I took, I was doomed to go around in circles.

Ironically, it was through this initial perspective that came a much more three-dimensional one.

The year I began writing this book, I was working as an extra on a film set. To say there was a group of personalities would be an understatement. Reminiscent of my schooling days. However, there was one guy in particular who I took a significant interest in. He was both shy and awkward, yet loud and obnoxious at the same time. Edging his way on the outs, whilst trying to become accepted as a part of the conversation. The more I reflected on it, I came to the sudden realisation that maybe this was perhaps the way I had come across to those around me. Was I just imagining all these unpleasant things or did I really act this way? Were the ways others treated me actually warranted? Thinking further, I contemplated the possibility that things can actually be seen as the other way round, as it is only you as the individual that controls your actions. You perceiving it to be that way, only creates the circumstances that reinforce it back onto you and then others. You are shy, introverted and insecure because they treat you that way, but they treat you that way, because you are shy, introverted and insecure. It works both ways. This cycle continues on a loop round and round, with each party involved waiting for the other to change. Yet neither ever do.

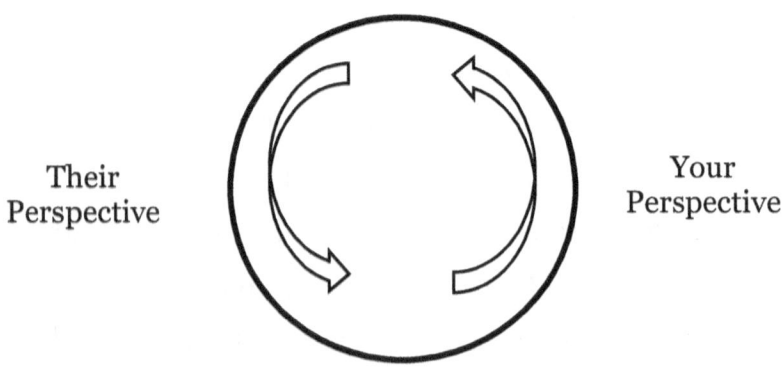

The Ultimate Principles
i.e., How To Break The Cycle

These principles are ones that are universal and not created to serve as a human construct. They take precedence above all notions, both existing and working independently of human influence. They do not work around you, so it is you who must work **with** them, using these as the foundation to all your subsequent actions.

A workable principle may initially be something that inspires motivation or thought. One that alters your awareness from what once was, to a higher level that invites transformation. In turn with this, you must learn to discard the secondary distractions, thought processes, relationships and habits that have kept you in this false state till now. Only then will you be able to replace them with new alternatives. With that said, take note of this first principle.

1. You cannot control the outcome when others are involved.

No matter how deeply we desire, we cannot control how others think, feel and act. Often, we blame others for our situation, but forget to acknowledge our influence in the eventual outcome. It is very easy to believe we come across the way we want to, that others will and should understand what we want them to hear and see. However, it is one thing to want; it is completely another thing to **know** how our persona to received. We can only control what we have control over. Ourselves. The way we think, feel, act and react to a situation.

This leads into the second principle.

2. In order to change your exterior world, you must first change the way you see things internally.

It is commonplace for people to believe that, "If I just get this, or change that, then things will automatically become better". Yes, they may, for an initial moment, however very soon you will realise things will find their way back to the same situation as before. Why?

These external extremities only mask what is really going on inside. Like a band aid, they cover up the wounds that cut deep internally. Like plaster, they act as a facade to the actual walls that tie directly to your true emotions.

Putting on a mask; Is that person genuinely you? Or genuine in its illusion?

When we put on a mask to others, it often is as a way to hide the dark insecurities of our own subconscious. As you will read in B*eing Honestly Vulnerable,* being real is to be honest, and through this real honesty comes truth. This is why looking introspectively within yourself and being accepting of your false actions is so important. It causes cracks in the façade to show. Having honest intention for a genuine purpose is the only way that things will change, and change permanently. More on that soon.

This then leads into the final principle.

3. *"**You cannot change the way you feel until you change the way you think, because your thoughts determine the way you feel**"*- Tony Evans

As we discussed with one thing affecting everything, the way you see yourself internally is greatly affected by the way you see yourself and the world around you. We know this is attributed to our habitus and past experiences, but interestingly by looking at this deeper, we see this creates a never-ending paradox. A cycle where the way you think towards something is determined by what you see in it, and what you see in something is determined by what you think.

The way you react to things determines the way you ultimately feel towards them.
Or
The way you feel toward things is determined by the way you react to them.
Simply put;
You **feel** this way, because you **think** this way.
You **think** this way, because you **feel** this way

So, change your thinking towards a situation, and naturally, you will change the way you feel about it. How though? A concept which requires you to think a certain way, is determined by something that ultimately will always have a pre-conditioned opinion/side. Well perhaps it isn't about having one?

How to Forgive Someone (Then Forget)

One day I crossed paths with a friend whom I went to school with. Immediately a memory opened up from a deep crevasse in my mind. I was sitting in IT class working on a major project, when suddenly I heard my name come up in conversation. I distinctly listened to his reply. "Don't worry. It's just Justin. Nobody cares about him." Yes, it was probably true, maybe they didn't care about me. Maybe he had just said it to make himself feel a part of the group.

Maybe I was indeed the verbal punching bag for the end of a joke. Then I stopped to look at it from the other perspective, referring back to the film set. That person was just trying to belong. Not only within the group, but within himself. The way he did that, was to seek approval from others. His problem was he was trying too hard. Having been in his situation countless times before, I understood where he was coming from. I understood he was simply trying to find a sense of self in a group where 'self' was selective. Therefore, I did not treat him like they treated me. I saw him as a person with their own fears, worries and pain. I saw him as I would have liked to have been seen.

There is no need to have hatred towards others for how they might have or are treating you. It is all irrelevant. In regards to that comment in class, I might have cared then, but I didn't now. I understood it from his perspective. I understood it from my own. The cycle had been broken. In hindsight, and through my exploration of self, I understood that they are just like I was. They were probably dealing with their own problems and insecurities, with their actions a way of deflecting their doubts onto you. That's why most relish in your fear. You reacting in the way they hope you would, only proves that their treatment of you is valid. It works in making them feel better about their situation. Only through understanding that the answer lies much closer to heart, will you be able to handle people like this. By knowing you are in the higher position, looking down on someone who is still acting through their false-self. In most instances, you should feel sorry for them.

Note: Now of course, there are different situations that hold much more prejudiced circumstances. While it doesn't always mean their actions were justified or right, take these principles as a framework to address it at its core. Remember the quote on page 26. You will find the same applies here.

The Cycle Breaks With You!

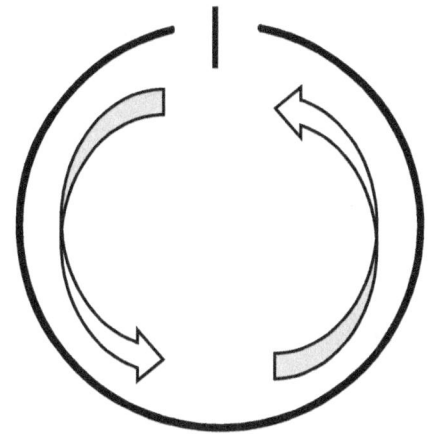

In our youth we seem so caught up on what others think of us. Then, as time goes by, we have so many new priorities and things that occur in our life, that we actually have no time to think about others. We realise that perhaps they weren't thinking about us at all, and even if they were, it was only for a moment. Then that moment is gone, and they go back to worrying about what others think.

You will find they care of you as much as **you think** you do of them.

If we hold onto our bitterness through adulthood, it only preserves the level of anxiety that we had as children. Your hatred towards another should never form to the point where you aren't aware you are actually doing more damage hating yourself. This is not as unfortunate as it appears, for now at a higher sense of awareness and understanding through your true-self, you can use this as an opportunity to look inside yourself and question. Your calmness towards the situation will in turn relay onto them. When their desired effect does not work on you, they may begin to question their own actions. In that brief moment, they realise the extent of their effects and like you, use that insightful moment to then look inside themselves. They may try another attempt to see if this was a one-off, but as long as you keep this knowledge in mind, and act without anger or haste, you will defuse any issue before it can gain traction.

"Forgive others, not because they deserve forgiveness, but because YOU deserve peace"- Jonathan Lockwood Huie

As Mahatma Gandhi once said; "Forgiveness is the attribute of the strong". I say it is the product of your true self in motion.

Different Viewpoints:
Branching Out Your Awareness

We view things as they present themselves to us. Surface level. One-dimensional. Mainstream media and commercialism are based on this principle. Sex sells. Wealth and power dominate. The temptations that reflect the belief that what you want is easily obtainable. It is through this sea of instant-gratification that we can lose our ability to see the underlying truths that are hidden beneath the surface. As a consequence, these 'realities' cause us to develop a fantasy, seeing only what we want to see, as opposed to what is really there. If we are to seek change across multiple avenues in our life, we must first **raise our awareness** to determine how we interact with what that fantasy actually is, as opposed to what it represents to us. With that said, like most things in this world, we can view our perspectives from one of two ways.

Narrow Viewpoints: Where your depth of vision is only limited to a very small width. 'Tunnel vision'. Straight and fine cut.

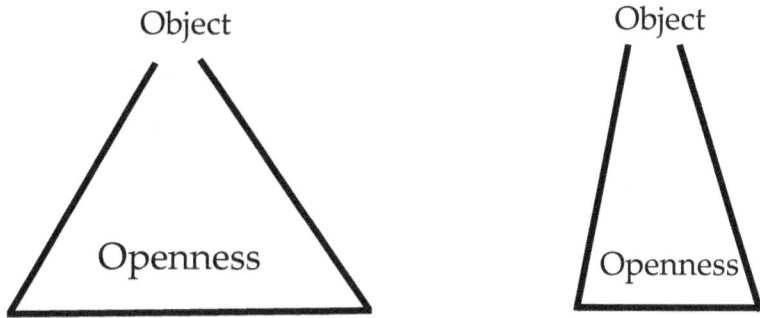

Worldly Viewpoints: Your perspective is not limited to your vision around you. Think 'outside the box', or what is beyond your immediate sight.

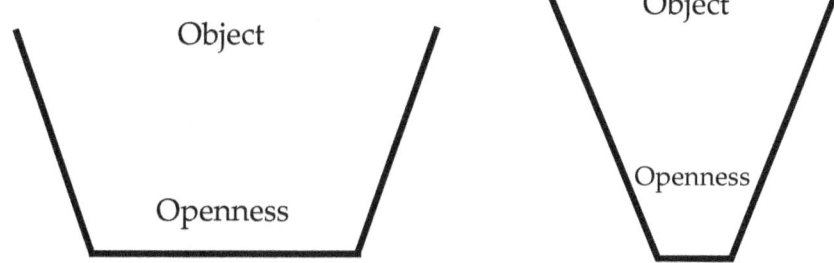

One Dimensional: The Power of Editing

We are all aware that practically every form of multi-media is edited together to create a certain feel and look. In most cases, it can be the make or break on whether the show succeeds or fails. However, perhaps we don't know the extent that it can go to, not only in shaping a particular message, but our perception of what that message is. For example, it is very possible to create a documentary about a horrific topic or person and shape it to make him/her seem sympathetic, misunderstood or right in what they were doing. Now, by no means is this appropriate, but it is that controversial hook to catch the unsuspecting worm that is our undivided attention. In that split moment our minds lose focus on what was, to what is, and the context along with it. Yes, we are consciously watching it, but are we aware of the effects that this may have on our self-conscious? The next time you come across a video that has a one-dimensional title, transform it so it says the opposite, or better yet, so it has none. You might be surprised as to what will discover, free of preconceived notion and thought.

Dealing With A 'Crush'

Take this scenario which I'm sure you have experience in your life (or perhaps am now). A crush. Whether you know them indirectly or directly, there is something about them that you are drawn to. I have had numerous 'crushes' over the years, none of which ever amounted to anything, however there was one in particular that opened up my eyes to a higher perspective. I was in my senior year of high-school. She in her junior. We would interact together once a week in this program known as 'house families' (where people across multiple year groups would get together). Immediately drawn to her beauty and warmth, I saw the potential of what 'could be'. Now of course, being the shy, awkward person that I was, this was as far as it went. Always admiring. Never taking action. With that, I falsely assumed that would be the last I saw of her.

Fast-forward a few years, I was now in my third year of college. Another year of failed ventures, rejection and lack of answers, I was on my way to a lecture, when, out of my peripherals, there she was. Immediately, those thoughts that had once flooded my mind, came rushing back. "Hm, I thought, small world". Returning from my class, my conscious was no longer concerned with what had transpired an hour ago, as surely, she would have gone. No. She was still there, now standing amongst the sea of people that had fanned out from the auditorium. About to turn my gaze, I was startled when she looked straight at me. I waved. Just a friendly gesture in response to our past. She did the opposite however, looking away. I couldn't believe it. It was in that moment, any sort of attraction I may have had over the years disappeared. Abolished. Gone. It made me wonder what I was even attracted to in the first place? We see the good in things, the potential in situations and people, which is a noble quality to have, yet by seeing only it from one perspective, you forget the role the other person plays. Remember the ultimate principles. By removing our gaze from this narrow field of view, we eradicate any jaded association we may have with this person. Now looking back, from her perspective, as most likely in my unsureness, I came across as an annoyance. Now, the tables had turned. The facade in which I had consumed my subconscious in for all that time, saw her not as one-dimensional, but a fully-fledged person. In a completely different light other than my own. This solution will be expanded upon in later chapters (See the sections; *Dealing with Rejection, How to be Truly Attractive,* & *Dating Flow*). In the case for worldly viewpoints, there will be times where, in order to truly understand a topic, you may need to pinpoint the finer details of things. However, when you are only focusing on one aspect of the situation, a wider perspective with an array of options is needed to open your eyes. For me, this was the case for my dream and my overarching goal. I knew where I wanted to go and what I wanted to do. The vision was there. Yet, coming out into the real world, I had no idea how to get there.

Joining Them Together

These viewpoints, although different in direction, are one of the same. They can all function in harmony. The key is to **view them in the right context.** Take narrow viewpoints. On one hand this can be beneficial to those striving to achieve a goal. That is all they see and nothing will steer them clear of that path (however that in itself has flaws). On the other, it can be extremely restricting when addressing the bigger picture. That is all they see, will see, and will be, without any attempt to broaden their perspective. Sometimes, this is because they know no better. Too stubborn. Held back by years of habit. Viewing things as a whole allows you to see things for as they are, rather than what you want them to be. It is as if every possible viewpoint co-exists simultaneously. This may require some further exploration into the reality of things, yet is absolutely necessary. So, the next time you see a form of media, look at a certain person, or even your doubt your thoughts.

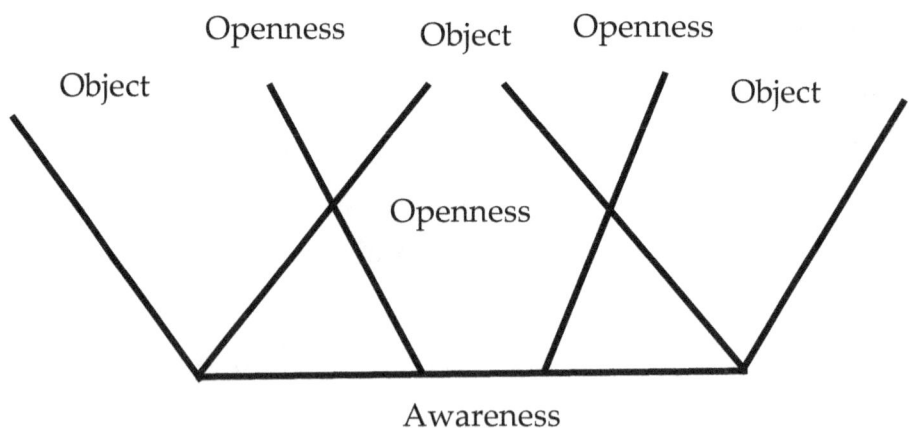

Pause. Ask why. Look deeper. Then do it again. Then again. Then again. Until you no longer need to.

How To Defeat Addiction

When first setting off into the unknown that was my introspective transformation, there was another question besides addressing self-guilt that I desperately needed answers to. How to Conquer Unwanted Habits.

As I talked about in my opening chapter on habitus and past experiences, the constant outcome of rejection and subsequent feelings of loneliness led me to find comfort in other areas, in particular through means of romanticism. Films, video-games, and later, pornography.

I could make a whole separate book on this if I wanted, as I know there will be many people (particularly males) reading this who currently are affected by this vice. However, although there are many types of addiction, be it video games, alcohol, food, pornography, drugs or smoking, they are in essence one of the same. Rather serving as forms that addiction can be structured to. You may not have the same as I once did (I know things affect people in different ways) but I do have experience in going through the cycle, and know people who have at some stage been involved with destructive habits. All I can offer you is my insight and the principles I used that allowed me to break free.

It All Starts with A Choice

Before I started writing this book, I came across an interview between the actor of the Sitcom, *Friends* fame, Matthew Perry, and BBC journalist Peter Hitchens. In this controversial discussion, Perry and Hitchens were debating their views surrounding drug addiction and courts, and whether they should enforce stronger penalties to those caught dealing and consuming.

Due to my ethical morals, and perhaps my familiarity with his work, I initially took side with Perry, who himself had struggled with addiction as a result of his fame. Whilst not facing drug addiction, I understood the feeling of having seemingly no control over my urges. Hitchens came across as pompous, arrogant, and with no lack of remorse or empathy towards those affected by drugs. He exclaimed brashly; "Addiction does not exist. It is rather a choice. It all starts with a choice".

Like Perry, I was taken back by this apathetic remark. How could an opinion on such a topic be this bias? How could someone possibly be led to think this way? Each person was on a 'side' for this and against that, attacking the other with bitterness and shock at what they had to say. "Why can't you see the way I see it?" The whole format of the interview was set up to cause conflict. Now without conflict things can become boring, but with conflict, we can be so taken back by the bias we can either be implored to investigate further, or so defensive that we make no solution of any kind.

I'm sure you agree, all addictions start off as distractions. New and exciting in your curiosity they provide a release from the pressures of life. Whether introduced through a group or by yourself to belong, they quickly become part of a repetitive cycle. A habit engraved into your subconscious that can be brought upon without thinking.

In my case, I would come home feeling tired, depressed and overwhelmed with my situation, and used these 'distractions' to ease the pain. I became reliant on them, shortly letting it become a habit. This then, lead to addiction. And so, started a chain reaction that kept me locked in a downward spiral of day to day, week to week, to month to year monotony. During the period where I would say my vice had its greatest hold on me, I would go through the following cycle. I would break free for a few days, then a week, then a month, only for the same feelings of isolation and loneliness to return. Addiction is not solely attributed to the item itself. Addiction is a state of mind in which you fall into. A clever trap that, without awareness and understanding, will isolate you even further.

Software Vs. Hardware

In researching for a wider perspective on different addictive structures, I came across an interview with Dick Van Dyke, on the *Dick Cavett Show*. I recommend it to any suffering alcoholic willing to heal. He not only provides firsthand experience, but clear reasoning why and how it affects you. I took note of this one comment by Van-Dyke.

"There is no pre-drinking morbid psychology in an alcoholic. It happens as a result of his physical addiction".

Some people are physically susceptible towards types of addiction. Meaning their body reacts to in a certain way that only exacerbates the effects. One drink becomes another then another and so on. These vices act not only a depressant, but a stimulant, created to do nothing more than target the weakness in your mind. The more you participate in the practice, the more the body adapts to the addiction, and vice versa. Although not an alcoholic, I took great attention to this. I like to think of it similar to that of software and hardware, and the definite way in which addiction to vices can affect an individual.

<u>Software:</u> Both subconsciously and consciously reprograms your brain to a new set way of thinking.

<u>Hardware:</u> Damages the physical components of your brain that allows for productive thought to occur.

Initial use temporarily reprograms your brain with new software (feeling of euphoria), while too much use over time will cause brain damage to the hardware. The comparison can be made to mental illness. There are diagnoses that are directly attributed to the physical components of the brain affecting the way the software runs. It is this damage to the hardware, that causes the software to become ineffective to reprogramming. All depression and anxiety do is act as instigators for people in choosing vices that lead to addiction. Over-time they subtly reprogram the brain's natural way of thinking to the extent where the individual has fallen so far down the rabbit hole, it no longer becomes a hole, but a cavern, with no light to guide the way.

So, on better inspection, Hitchens is right. It is a choice. Everything starts as one. The difference, which through his indifferent demeanour, (of perhaps the context of the interview), could not understand, is that in some cases, they do not make the choice through direct consciousness. We get so caught up in our despair, consumed by our habitual ways, and the effects of these addictions, that the line between making that choice is near non-existent. I believe this was the underlying message Perry was openly conveying.

You will find it is not so much about stopping the addiction flat out, but stopping the ability to having the first one. Again, it all starts with a choice.

What Things Can I Do to Stop the First?
Environment and Boredom

You may initially think, "If I just change my environment, then things will change". Yes, it might, at first, but just as your mind has adjusted to subconscious programming, those destructive habits will adjust too. Your distractions will try to find a way back as you start to become comfortable. Now by environment I mean two types. The first being the building, room or area where you are most likely to give in, the obviously solution here being to avoid/remove yourself entirely from them. The second, is referring to your current situation overall. Addictions can also arise out of boredom, a symbolic reminder for the lack of excitement in your life. In order to rival this, you need other tasks, to distract you from your own distractions. Ones that are so constructive, the more you delve into them, the sooner they become your new addiction. (See *Lack of Motivation/Excitement*).

Use Branching Awareness

A part of being addicted, is where you are consciously taking part (be it watching, eating, smoking or drinking) in it, but to the point where you no longer are aware of the effects that this has on your self-conscious. I may have been consciously watching the images flickering on the screen, however it was as if I was unconsciously in a sort of limbo, where all feeling was lost. I had convinced myself that it was okay, for my betterment, when really there was nothing that was going through my mind in the first place. It was running blank.

Conscious - unconsciousness **or** unconscious - consciousness

This is the crossroad for your vice to either cease living, or flow over into excess. You may say, "I can stop. All it takes is a split-second decision", yet this is just a way of denying its hold. To save face and self-guilt by blaming others rather than the illusion that is ourself. An effective method is to view these thoughts as just being that. Thoughts. Then, you offset these thoughts with another. One that disproves the justification of why the addiction should exist. Understand the parameters by which your vice is built upon. Ultimately, it is a product designed to target weakness, and you are just a pawn taking part in their plan to get ahead for themselves. The more people participate, the wider its influence it has on society as a whole. Whenever the urge came across me, I took a moment to think of all the pros and cons of me doing this addiction, skipping ahead as if I had already indulged in it. Immediately I discovered it is much easier to negate feelings associated with the aftermath, when there is a lack of feeling to be had in the first place. Only when we acquire the essence of what our addiction was initially used for, we end up realizing we no longer have a use for them.

The Art of Non-Identification

The final piece that allowed me to break free of my vice, was understanding I had to break my perception of them. Ask yourself why you are really doing it? Deep down you know it is wrong, but you justify it by associating 'coping' as a way to making yourself feel better.

- It helps me feel better about myself
- It's okay if I give in. Everyone else does it!

This isn't about others; this is about YOU! Having this attitude only reinforces the negative self and habitual thinking that got you here in the first place. It will continue to keep you there on repeat unless you first become aware of the damage that it is doing to you. Unfortunately, that is something no amount of information from an outside source can do. It comes from within.

On the opposite end of the spectrum, we know this is doing us harm, and we pile on the guilt. "Oh, I did that because I am lonely. A loser. My life is horrible". By identifying yourself as part of the problem, we only reinforce the vice's hold. We let it stay for another bite. Vernon Howard has a great passage on what he identifies as **non-identification**.

"You break the habit by ceasing to identify with it. To identify with a habit means that you take the habit as yourself- but you are not the same thing as your habit. You may have the habit of wearing a green jacket, you are not the same thing as that jacket; you are merely wearing it for a time. Likewise, you are not the same thing as your habit. You and your habit are two entirely separate things."

In my desperate efforts to resist, I failed to realise it was this that was the crux of the whole battle. By calling it a battle, I was identifying it. By calling it a battle, I was acknowledging its existence, and thus, hold over me. As soon as I ceased fire with all thoughts and language associated with my vice, it laid down its arms and waved the white flag of peace. I realised then and there, addiction isn't something we don't defeat or abolish. It is something we accept. Accept through the understanding and self-knowledge of ourselves. Accept to the point, where there is nothing left to accept. From then on, I never felt the urge, because I didn't know there was an urge to be had. The thought never crossed my mind.

Time Is Irrelevant

We often judge our success with our addiction through means of counting years. The first time we decide to make a change for ourselves, it is usually the result of a particular life-changing moment. One that shocks us so much, it allows us to see the light. Whether it be the death of a family member as a result of the same addiction, or the birth of a child, we think because of these events, it will be easy to stop. The longer time passes, the more we believe we are immune to the temptations.

A week into completing this section, I had become increasingly aware of the lack of excitement in my life. Editing a book is a long, arduous process, and for someone who naturally lacks present focus and patience, this eventually took its toll. I fell back into my distractions of habit, then my vice. Deep down I knew this was wrong, and even though I didn't fall victim to its effects fully, it was in that split second, I had an epiphany. It was at this exact point the first time I started this journey. The coping through distractions. The lack of discipline. The mundane environment. I could have easily fallen back into the rabbit hole of non-existence that had buried me once before. You could go for one, five, ten, even twenty years without indulging in your vice, however the split moment you take the advantage to light that cigarette, swallow that drug, or press play, you have just wasted all that hard work. The cycle has started again.

Unless you truly understand your vice, to see that it isn't a vice but rather your problems associated with it, you can break that cycle. I could either dwell in it feeling guilty or acknowledge what I had done. Finally, I remembered my goal (refer to page 149). I had something that, even though it was available to me before, provided a clear path that was foreseeable. An item that was a symbolic reminder that I had no reason to give up. This book was that item. Plus, my work didn't save. I guess that's what I get.

Life Is A Rollercoaster:
A More Active Perspective

Many see life through the roller coaster metaphor; Like a rollercoaster. Lots of ups and downs. Now this is true. Life does have its good times and bad, most often with events we have no control over; however, I believe that there is a deeper meaning that can be explored to this perspective. One from a more active approach. As you have picked up this book, it is clear to say you feel as if your life is going nowhere. You feel stuck, in a constant cycle of rinsing and repeating; (the better metaphor would probably be a washing machine). If this is indeed the case, perhaps it is safe to say that it is more likely caused by a passive outlook. Rather than accepting this as what life has to offer, we must inquire into the events we have an influence on, both directly and indirectly. Ultimately, we must ask how does this contribute to the current state of our existence? What mindset does this represent?

Are we being pulled along on its set track? Are we the passenger? The driver? Or the next person in line at the queue?

Deep down people have the desire and will to change. They think, "Right! This will be the year, or month or week". Yet they soon realise through this simplicity in thinking comes a complexity in doing, and they are back telling themselves that exact phrase. In order to transcend this, we must delve deeper into process by which one can transcend themselves. By that I mean, gaining momentum.

Gaining Momentum

This is perhaps the most difficult ingredient in achieving your happiness. It is dependent on an aspect of yourself that you must constantly apply. Persistence. The ability to not give up and keep striving. Although at times you may believe it, that longing for change never goes away. It only gets silenced by outside variables that influence your thought. If you know deep down that you should make the change, then this should be the foundation to your mission of recovering your true self. A person who truly and deeply wants to change their current position, will. It is inevitable. It just takes time.

Once I started to become aware of and subsequently address the areas of my life that were dragging me down, I noticed an immediate change in my outlook and approach to my situation. It was as if suddenly new life had been injected into me. Not only did I have more energy and motivation to accomplish tasks, I was more present and accepting of where I was now. I had come from such a low state, that I had now returned to neutral ground. It is common place to believe the notion that success only comes when you are at your best. While yes, to a degree this is true, rather than envisioning the big goal ahead, take note on every little moment that comes our way and act on it through our authentic self. The goal that you attribute this romanticized version of success to, is built on the accumulation of small success every day. In order to be at your best, you first must simply be. Get to know who you are now, so you become what is required tomorrow.

The diagram below illustrates the many paths that momentum can take.

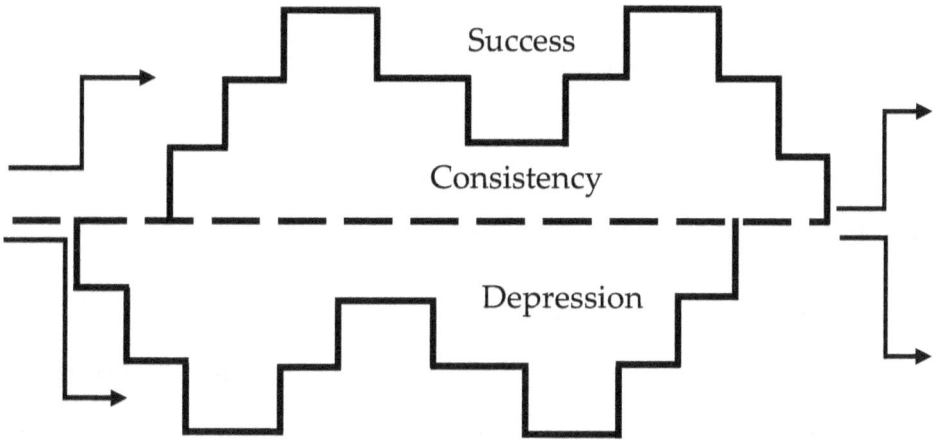

Below the Line

Below is where depression, bad habits and addiction settle in. The more years that pain and habit cover, the deeper the rabbit hole plummets. The further down you go, the more steps you have to climb to get out. With each stage you have to reset and regather your mind.

Above the Line

Above the line is a state of constant evolution. Other than reflecting your false self and negative thoughts, this state illustrates the effects of your personal development; strength, skillets and passions. Like a muscle, each time you do a task, the stronger your will power becomes. Even if you do fall, because it is from such a high state, the easier it will be to regather yourself.

Middle Line

This represents the middle line of existence where all things run along. A note to consider with this state is that it can occur both above the line, and below it. You become too passive and comfortable with your situation; your opportunities will grow stale. There will come a point in your transformational process where things will indeed go stagnate. This is an indication that you need to make a sudden change. To 'flip the script' (see page 146).

How to Move Up Each Step

Referring back to the principle that one thing effects everything, you have to study the aspects that hold direct accessible priority in your life. By doing so, you will become able to give only the amount which is required. Not so little that it does not equate to anything, and not to extent that you are consumed by it. So, ask yourself.

- What areas can I take a break from that causing me to spiral?
- What areas can I explore that will put me on the path of growth?

Do a task that, instead of reflecting your false-self; negative thoughts and egocentric desires, is driven by your personal development. One that is an expression of your strengths, skills and passions. The more you succeed, the more it gives you reassurance that this is right.

Rather than seeing depression as a negative, a fire that will quickly eat away at you with its bad habits, turn it into something good. Use it as fuel to your own fire, to start the engine up again. All it takes is a change in outlook and understanding. Whenever you fall back into a terrible state, realise that this a way of the universe telling you that you need to change gears and take the next step.

Think of it as hitting a wall that then gives you a warning to turn around. If your path is more difficult, it is because your calling is higher. It is where all the obstacles are guarding the prize. It isn't going to be laid out so you can simply walk up and retrieve it. From the outside this can be quite overwhelming and off-putting, and most people who start will fail before they can truly get going. Take it hour by hour, day by day. Engrave the habit into your behaviour. In order to have consistent momentum to grant success, you must commit yourself to the process, lose all distractions, and create a simplified routine to follow. One of a particular structure that works to your advantage and creates only positive action. As you will later learn in exploring your interests, if you are passionate about something, your drive to do it is unsurpassed. It symbolizes your true-self slowly emerging from the embers of the flame.

A More Active Perspective

So now we have broken down the metaphor of our favourite carnival ride, it is safe to concluded that there needs to be more active perspective to our approach. How though? There is only so much one can do on a rollercoaster. Well then, how about we don't see it in the constraints it presents to us. See life, better yet, as a **balancing act**. A constant state of keeping things in harmony;

controlling the things you can and not stressing on the things you cannot. When you recognise a sudden intake of bad, you instantly shift the balance by taking in what is good for you.

> *"Absorb what is useful, reject what is useless, and add what is essentially your own"* - Bruce Lee

This mantra forms the basis for the entire self-transformational process. Not only is this entire book a drawn-out version of this concept, but as you read every single chapter, you will absorb the knowledge that you find relevant in favour of discarding your current way of thinking, adding your interpretation by the only way you know how.

Sometimes you can go through the twists and turns of the rollercoaster and come out not wanting to ride again, but if you can understand **why** you wanted to in the first place, then all that sorrow will be but a leaf in the wind.

ACT II

In Order To Move On From Where You Have Come:
You Must Know to Where It Is You Are Going

Now that you have accepted your past events and emotions associated with them, you are able to focus on where you need to be presently for the future. Aware to the existence of your true self versus your false self, you have to take that knowledge and relate it back to your life as it is. This means figuring out where you want to go.

"What if I don't know that? What if I have no idea who I want to be or what I want to do"?

I come across people who say this phrase all the time. My reply is always the same. "What interests do you have?"
"I don't know?"

You do know. You have always known. Without needing an explanation, you are drawn to certain styles, genres and looks. As we discussed earlier, this is partly due to your habitus and cultural preconditioning through childhood, but to take a deeper look, this is your true self speaking to you.

Consuming myself purely through a romanticized view of the world, allowed me to escape and find existence from a place where I felt constantly trapped within myself and around others. Being a libra (not that I put my faith in horoscopes), I have always been attracted to things that are remotely creative. Art. History. Pop-culture. Movies. You name it. I know I get this interest from my mother, and the one thing it gives me is variety, but I also believe heavily that everything has to have balance, even in its unbalance (more on that later).

How Big Is Your World?

Despite knowing the world is a vast and epic as it is, ask yourself, how aware am I to the relation this has towards my own place in it? If you were to map out the various places you go to in one, five, or maybe even ten years, you will slowly realise the difference between 'the world that is', and the world the you have created/been subjected to. For example, if you are cooped up inside all day at home or work, the world that is available to you is one of little grandiose. By broadening our awareness internally, we are able to generate the possibility that there is something bigger out there. Something, that can only be created through our own exploration. When we use the phrase 'to the whole world', rarely are we referring to those in our immediate surroundings. The world is as big as you see it. How much we see is limited to how much we know, and how much we know is determined by how much we see in it.

In setting out to implement a change in our life or chase our big dream's, we either have one of these paradoxes swimming around in our subconscious. (Refer back to branching awareness).

1. We know the end destination, but become overwhelmed with a lack of direction or path.
2. We know the path, yet lack the tools or method to get started.
3. We have the tools, yet have no idea where to go and how to utilize them.
4. We have no idea about the tools, path and goal altogether.

We fixate on the goal to the extent where we lose the opportunity to accumulate the tools. When we don't have the tools, we lose direction and our path becomes narrower. We become stuck, grow stagnate, and then give up. It is not necessarily the lack of tools that halt our progress, but our perception and thought process towards what is needed at the current moment. Some say it is not about the goal, but path. I say it is the successful combination of all. Tools. Path. Goal. It all depends on the context in which you implement them cohesively. The goal is continuing on the right path, the pathway, is going from skillset to skillset. The tools, could be the goal that you need right at this very moment.

They all relative in their relativity, meaning for some, the starting point may be having the end goal, and for others the end goal, may be accumulating the right tools. You don't have to know the end destination; all that is needed is a starting point. Having an initial interest gives you this point. An inkling of what you want to be and where you want to go. For some it can start with a certain topic or area of expertise. As you explore it, and delve deep into the process of doing, you will automatically find opportunities presenting themselves. Opportunities you thought were never possible. No matter how small at first, an interest still holds potential. The potential to hold possibility. (Read *Pathways: Job, College, Career*).

Your Notion of Success

Society worships those who succeed. Those who seem to be on that higher 'unattainable level'. This is, because to us, they represent that aspect of life that we can only dream to achieve. As touched on previously, what one sees is determined by what is around them, and with the constant subjection to what society deems as successful through others, our own aspect of life becomes extremely warped and clouded. So much so, when we are asked by others what our notion of success is, we are given in to providing one of these answers.

"Money. Fame. Being the best. Achieving the highest level".

The fateful mistake people make in chasing their dreams, is that they see a successful person, and decide to mimic and copy them and their path. They believe that it is the accumulation of the external reputation and materialistic riches that defines success.

This approach can only take one so far. Even if you attain these things, you will find the novelty of success will slowly fade, and you will be brought back to the reality of your own problems. Yes, these people may have all these things, and temporarily be happy, but if you were to sit them down and ask them how they were internally? Most likely (but not always), they would be far from **content** and **fulfilled.** Nothing will have changed because their intention was not based on something honest. We trick ourselves, saying it is for our best interest. It is for myself. To be liked. To get money. To be successful. To have a better life. As you will discover throughout your introspective transformation, having honest intention is the only **true way** that will allow for longevity in one's self. Desire is a word that comes with a lot of confusion when talking about success. What do all these desires have in common? They are all based in ego-centric origins. (See B*ecoming the Person You Tried Not to Be: You and Your Ego)*. While yes, all these may in fact bring you those things, they are brought about by your ego, and thus a part of your false-self. I remember I was asked this same question of success in my senior year of english studies. Naturally, those around me presented the above answer, saying there is no point doing something unless it is for the highest level. I gave a different approach.

> "Not necessarily. For them, what they are willing to achieve is at the highest level. That may just be the best version of themselves. For others, it may be to strive for the best, because it is in their capability. It all depends".

In regards to this book, I would hope it has the potential that I can take it to its highest level. To not to, would be a disservice to the overall message. Whatever follows as a result however, would be a bonus.

A Role Model

Most of the successful, confident people that you look up to and draw inspiration from, never seem to act by their emotions. They are calm, collected and always seem to come out of the situation no worse for wear. In the movies this is a glamorized version of course, but given the right context, an actual life reflection of the true self in action.

Find a role model that summarizes you. A celebrity. A movie or comic-book character. Someone that you feel best reflects you in a nutshell. They may share the same values as you, symbolize a part of you that you aspire to be, or may have experienced the same pain and heartbreak similar to what you have. Having a role model or someone to look up to gives us reassurance that there are other people out who have similar stories who are able to come from nowhere to gain a better life for themselves (or succeed). The best is subjective. The best is based on **other** people. Most people who experience this top success given through others, still long for acknowledgment within themselves.

It's Not How Tall You Stand

I remember once hearing that despite accomplishing his dream of being the number one champion fighter of the world, Muhammad Ali didn't actually enjoy boxing, but was more appreciative for what it did for him. Finding this quite dumbfounding, how could, who is regarded as the greatest boxer all of time, not relish the sport that he dominated in? I admit initially, from the interviews that I saw of him, he came across as a loudmouth, arrogant, selfish person proclaiming; "I am the best". However, as I researched deeper into his life, learning how he stood up for his religious views, to his refusal to serve in the military (resulting in the loss of his title and boxing license), I slowly understood what his actions illustrated. It was a way for him to reassure himself and others that no matter what society threw at him, he was doing the right thing. Every aspect of the sport was a way of expressing and communicating his true self. The resilience to stand up for what he believed was right. To go against what was expected of him. He inspired so many people around the globe because of this, not just because he was a skilled boxer. That is why he is seen in such high regard. That is why he was the greatest. For what he stood for. Plight and perseverance are, in the long run, always more appreciated than the accolades. Just make sure these carry across all aspects of your life.

It is not how tall you stand, but what you stand for, that counts. What do you stand for? A greater good? Or a lesser limitation of self?

Self-Honesty & Genuine Intention

This rule is one that is perhaps the most in depth to understand when it comes to our longing to change. On the one hand, it can easily be the defining factor in uncovering sincerity of truth. On the other, it can be open for hollow misinterpretation. Therefore, it is crucial to distinguish the difference between **intention** and **motivation**. For example, let's use a common scenario that might provide someone to want to change.

Someone calls you fat (or skinny in my case).

This what is known as the **insightful moment** that affects you on a level deep enough to question; why me? Like the desire to change, you are simply fed up. Reached your breaking point. However, with genuine intention, this desire to change provides not only the reason, but the foundation for everything else that will follow as a result. This insightful moment then leads you to your intention; TO CHANGE YOURSELF. Motivation is something that keeps you going. That drive. Often the two are mixed up in order, with the motivation acting as the intention. This will only lead to a false sense of accomplishment. With motivation acting as your intention, you automatically put expectations on the outcome. An outcome that is dependent on others. Even if you reach that goal, it is a goal that is built on spite, a grudge or negative thinking towards someone. You think; "I'll show them. If I do this, they will then respect me and see what they were missing". There is no guarantee that they will see you in a new light. Often, they only see the grudge or bitter feelings that have served as the foundation for this 'change'.

With that said, whenever thinking of doing something, ask yourself; What is my intention with this? Am I being lazy? Am I acting out of malice? What is the outcome I hope to achieve? Ask yourself this every time you do something. Soon, it will become habit. Without thinking. It is as your conscious is there on your shoulder, providing immediate response to your internal thought. (See *How to Read the Situation & Act Accordingly*).

All successful change (both enduring and evolving), is built on honest intention.

How To Deal With Rejection

Rejection hurts. Plain and simple. It is not our initial preference to be on the receiving end of someone saying no. It symbolizes we are not good enough. Not attractive enough. Not up to the standards one holds when deciding whether or not to create a deeper connection. The worst thing is, we often don't get these answers by the person themselves, and thus fall into a state of anxiety, and later, depression. All the time playing it back in our heads wondering where we went wrong. I wish I could say myself, I was used to it, but after almost a decade of the same outcome, you realise it is something you do not deal with, but rather accept.

"What? Accept? I am just supposed to wallow in my self-pity?"

Not wallow. Emerge from.

Although we equate our experience in being rejected as something entirely associated to the individual, it is actually the other person's shoes one must put themselves in to understand the circumstances surrounding why they may have done so.

1. Not that into you

If they aren't feeling it, then why pursue it? This creates a prolific thought that is far more vital. What vibe are you giving off to warrant this rejection? (See *How to Be Truly Attractive*).

2. They just want to work on themselves.

The person in question is conflicted in what they are after and overwhelmed in processing so much. Just respect it. Again, this something they aren't sure about, usually is themselves, and therefore you can't control. Some may say this as a passive-aggressive way of breaking things off with you. Ironically, this actually indicates it is definitely you who needs to work on yourself.

3. Taken

Upon meeting someone, we immediately create a grand set of expectations is our head of how we want this to pan out. We get that rush of excitement and surge of emotions just by talking to them. I can only assume that you have had these words said to you at some stage of your life; "You come across too strong". "It was only natural", you say. Yes, from your perspective it may seem that way, but I guarantee if you were to view the same situation again from an outside perspective, you would realise that although it seemed natural, it was built on this foundation of needing gratification (remember branching awareness and crushes). Now yes, people can be mean, not upfront and dishonest, but ask yourself; would you do the same thing in his/her shoes? Now initially you say no, being the empathetic person you are, but as you grow and develop, you too will be put in this situation where you may have to potentially 'reject someone'. (See page 71).

The Equation

In regards to my rejection, while on the surface, it appeared it was simply because they didn't like me, I still required more to develop my understanding of 'why'. Why was this happening to me? Why would things always end? Why was I not able to sustain anything? We are often taught in these situations to remember everything happens for a reason. That it was just a part of 'God's plan'. These approaches, designed to provide some comfort, only provide answers on a superficial level. These false expectations that I would often generate, were dependent on so many different variables in order to happen. I started to think about it from another perspective, one that removed all the one-dimensional vagueness, and combined the finer details of the situation. This led me to what I identify as *The Equation*.

You + Other + Time = Outcome

You

'You' refers to as both your mindset and approach.

The Other Person

Where they are at in their stage of life, and the mindset they bring with it. Looking back, I was ironically so concerned with something that was entirely out of my control. As you cannot control the thoughts of others, there is no need to worry. There is a big difference between flat out rejection and simply not aligning with their current life situation.

Time

Time also refers to your current thought process or approach. If things don't amalgamate, then it means you simply aren't ready. It is a clear indication that you need to reflect on your actions, develop your character, and broaden your perspective.

This relates to not just rejection in relationships, but any context where you are held back, say career. Sometimes it is these harsh experiences that are designed to open up reality. Everything will happen as it was meant to eventually based on this equation. Some consider this destiny, or it happened for a reason. Perhaps it just happened, because it happened. It is all the same. This equation just gives a more tangible element to this. I do however, believe things, need to be resolved. No page left unturned. This may be years down the road, but none the less, a part of completing the equation. Things need to be brought full circle.

What If I'm Not Given Answers?

Don't expect answers. They very well could be unsure themselves, and simply not want the truth to hurt you. Though sometimes, it is this lack of truth, that actually does the damage. I have been subjected to my fair share of people acting as if I didn't exist. A lesser person not worthy of the truth. This impacted greatly on my self-confidence. However, when I was put in that position yourself, where someone was asking answers, I didn't see it as an attack. I just see them as someone confused and trying to process everything, just like I had. The difference that separates you from those who have rejected you, is that you have an understanding of being in that situation yourself. Therefore, you will respect them as a fellow human being, being completely honest and upfront, explaining why you feel this way, what vibe they are giving off in order for you to feel this way. Give them the respect and courtesy that you would need, and calmy tell them where your decision is coming from. Treat them like a human being. Not someone unworthy of the truth. They themselves could also be limiting their perspective through high standards and unrealistic expectations. If this is the case, you wouldn't want to be with that person anyway.

On the other end of the spectrum, some people may become hostile towards the rejector. Whilst trying to process things, they act passive-aggressive towards the other, demanding answers. This only scares them away, proving their reasons for rejecting them in the first place! These people too have to learn something though. In fact, it is the same principle that underlines your own transformation. All you hope, is that they too go through what you have. To understand the other side of the story. To experience humility.

With humility brings awareness. With awareness brings empathy. With empathy brings understanding.

Get it Out of Your System

By understanding why, it is you have been rejected, you will automatically bring things back to you and your influence. This means ridding yourself of your emotions so you are not able to act upon them. Behaviours built upon by emotion always lead to more pain. Do not do things to cope! Having these distractions which will later turn into habit, only reinforce the hurt you have gone through. Yes, this means to not surround yourself in watching romantic movies or listening to break up songs. We need a release, however if we just bottle it up, we are only acknowledging its hold.

Move On. Easier said than done. This is difficult as we tend to dwell on it. Why they rejected us. What you did wrong. If you just did this different or acted this way. Over and over in our minds. You can't! Yes, it sucks, but it is out of your control. Remember, the first *Ultimate Principle*; You cannot control how someone thinks feels and acts. If we open our awareness about this whole concept, we will realise that it makes much more sense for the following. That it is not the situation that is causing your feelings of despair, but your reaction to it.

Plenty Of Fish in The Sea

You have heard this saying many times before. As cliché as this phrase has become, it actually holds great solace in accepting rejection. If viewed from the right perspective, it can transform your approach into something of great tranquillity.

There were numerous times in my own experiences, when I would feel content and confident in myself and a situation would present itself where I met someone, had a conversation, only for them to be already involved. Instead of retreating back into a state of despair like I usually had done, only to instigate the cycle, I asked myself a simple question. Would I have attracted them if they weren't taken?

Clarity comes from accepting that each individual had their path of evolution to follow. Leave them happy in that moment. In some cases, things develop over time and others won't add up/happen when you want them to. Having genuine intention and subsequent action can influence this positively, but if it's not meant to be, then so be it. Maybe not now, but maybe, sometime down the track, they will present themselves again to you. Only this time you will allow yourself the level that naturally offers itself. No matter the situation. This is relative to sex and relationships. We put these on a pedestal, rather than understanding the primary feelings, emotions and intimacy that exists without labels. (See pages 105-107). You will soon find another that gives you that feeling, and the thought of that other person will slip away. In most cases, it's not the person that you miss, **it's the feeling they gave you.** I feel both the following passage from Thomas Merton's novel, *No Man Is an Island,* and this poem by Osho, best fit this notion.

> *The beginning of love is to let those we love be perfectly themselves, and not to twist them to fit our image.*
> *Otherwise, we love only the reflection of ourselves we find in them.*
>
> **And**
>
> *If you love a flower, don't pick it up.*
> *Because if you pick it up it dies and it ceases to be what you love.*
> *So, if you love a flower, let it be.*
> *Love is not about possession. Love is about appreciation.*

Appreciating who they are, what their essence is, and how they hold themselves, even if those same feelings are not returned reciprocally.

Being Alone vs. Feeling Lonely

A scenario that became a common occurrence to me, was whenever I wanted to be alone, there were always people around, and whenever I felt the need for companionship, there was no one who had no interest in socializing. I am sure you too have had this same feeling of loneliness. The worst part is the more it happens, the more it impeaches on your sense of self, alienating you further. In most cases it is this isolation that has directly caused our feelings of seclusion to surface. You retreat deep into yourself and your feelings, not knowing that it is your thinking and approach towards it that is driving these outcomes. You get to the point, where the only person you can find solace in is yourself. All you have left is what you began with.

Let me tell you that it does not have to be this way. Not in a preachy sense to fit the context of this book, but because literally it does not. That is the first thing you must know about this concept. There is a phenomenal difference between **feeling lonely** and **being alone**. You can easily separate the two and change your state of being, by understanding, then knowing how to practically apply it.

Origins of the Two

While both are seemingly different, being lonely and being alone/aloneness derive from the same origins.

1. Rejection: Rejection from others, and subconsciously by yourself. It makes you think you are not good enough for them, inadequate, and that you can't provide what they require.

2. Lack of trust in self: Seeking the approval of others to fill that void you have within yourself will only end in further feelings of loneliness. It again reflects the subconscious confirmation that you are not good enough.

3. Need for companionship: We surround ourselves with this higher belief that in order to feel whole in within, we need another. Understandable, as everyone needs to feel wanted. That's what the idealized forms of media tell us. However, how can they be loved, when they haven't truly learnt to love themselves?

I'm sure you will agree no one wants to feel wanted simply because the other can't function by themselves. This dependency on others is a prime reason for being rejected, and thus create the reasons for you being alone and feeling lonely. (Remember the cycle of perception).

"Well, it is hard not to like it", you will say. "It sucks being alone and to be rejected". Yes, it does, but looking at the ultimate principles again, when it comes to others, we can only control what we as individuals put out and receive. For years I had wallowed in my aloneness thinking it was all I had, when it was all that, I needed.

Boredom & Procrastination

This comes directly as a consequence of loneliness and subsequently ending up on your own. As you have no one else around, all you have is yourself. This after a while, becomes incredibly lifeless and mind-numbing. Tasks have no substance and you constantly jump from one to the other in a careless run of dull procrastination.

In my instance, every-time I was either rejected, or in the process of dealing with my life situation, I would need numbing habits that only became mindless tasks where I wasted time. In order to fight this feeling of lonesomeness you need a hit of self-pleasure to reassure yourself, that "hey if no one else cares about you, the only person I can rely on is myself." Now this thinking is actually the correct, however the context and foundation on which it sits on leads to dissatisfaction. You need self-pleasure because you are lonely, because everything around indicates that this is all you are capable of receiving. If only you could see that by using self-pleasure to cope, you are actually reaffirming your loneliness. Deep down we know what we must do, but with a lack of direction and knowledge, we lose that level of excitement and passion needed in our lives to move forward. We have become comfortable. (Refer to the section: *Lack of Motivation/Excitement*).

Vernon Howard once stated that "The person with an enthusiasm for the truth about life need never worry about his enthusiasm for life".

I think this saying can be said the same for oneself as much as it does for life.

The person with an enthusiasm for the truth about themselves need never worry about their enthusiasm for themselves.

We confuse comfortability in our situation, to comfortability in ourselves. Often, we accept our situation, as a way of taking the pressure off our already overloaded conscious. Now that is indeed a part of the approach, to accept what is now in order to create what will become, but in this instance, they are one of the same. Your environment is a reflection of your mindset, and your mindset is a representation of your lifestyle. It is this stale cocoon we have concealed ourselves externally, that is the exact isolation we need to break free from internally.

You must get the point where you are comfortable within yourself to be able to attract the companionship that you were fixated on before. Although this time you no longer need it to survive.

How to Do This?

Going back to one of the first principles you have learnt. You are the only one living your life. **Be your own best friend first. Bring things back to you.** Fight it with an active task that will benefit you.

This may come across as being selfish, but let me reassure you, this is the most selfish-unselfish thing one can do for themselves. It is not selfish in the conventional term, because it does not chuck away concern for others for personal gain. It puts you first, for your personal growth. If you have the active intention of doing something for you, the response will give you feeling of closeness to your true self.

Here are some activities to complete in a sequence.

>Cleaning your room/Organising wardrobe

> Meditate (both static and active). (See meditation)

> Sport (Refer to process of self-learning)

>Playing music (Instrument or listening)

>Drawing or Painting (A project to constantly work on)

>Gym (Expression of the body through movement)

> Researching/reading (Gain knowledge to lead you into the next sequence)

As you progress through your journey, you will find the action of addressing comfortability something that constantly needs refinement. It is perfectly normal to fall back into this state numerous times. Learning how to balance these perfectly into a malleable routine will be the next step. (See *Flipping the Script*).

"I don't do any of those things?"

Well that just shows a lack enthusiasm in life. You need interests. Having interests gives multiple avenues to explore. To open up knew creative parts about yourself that you never thought you knew existed. Interests can start with just a thought; the important thing is to start. Research. Look at popular material to get inspired. (See *The Process of Self -Learning*).

This book itself is a task that symbolizes exactly the reasons I feel that written literature still holds precedent over digital mediums of the same content. By having someone else tell me these things, I became lost within the excess of information and pace of which the lecturer talked. It felt like that, a lecture. My mind was constantly jumping back and forth between the clutter of tone, diction, and in some cases music. It had no time to breath, sit, and wallow in the process of self-learning. Being able to sit alone, and focus on a task at your own pace, without multiple distractions is the reason why reading is so effective. I feel we have lost a part of ourselves, in the quest for instant satisfaction and monetary fulfilment.

Structured Perspective

As summarized in the chapter on narrow and worldly viewpoints, it is much more beneficial to have an open, assertive perspective than a closed off one. Obvious as this sounds, it ironic that despite the population being as diverse and never-ending as it is, people still follow one particular set of thinking. They limit themselves by positioning their beliefs into either one of these categories.

Left ——— Centre ——— Right

Now once again, we know this is all partially because of our habitus; our upbringing and morals, however whenever I ever came across someone with a controversial issue that wasn't the same as mine, it made me question. How can they see it that way? Conservative. Liberal. Libertarian. They all have strengths, weaknesses and merits giving a certain context, yet they can't be all right? Now the last thing I want to do is get political, as there is enough political confusion and noise swirling around in the world, but I believe by approaching such issues (as well as non-political) in a sequence, a common resolution can be made.

House Metaphor

Looking at it through a house metaphor, we are able to see through the notion that barriers only separate, that there is a better way. Instead of opposing one another in a constant state of debate/argument, the more proficient (albeit ideal) way of working together in harmony, is to each provide support to the other as part of an overarching sequence.

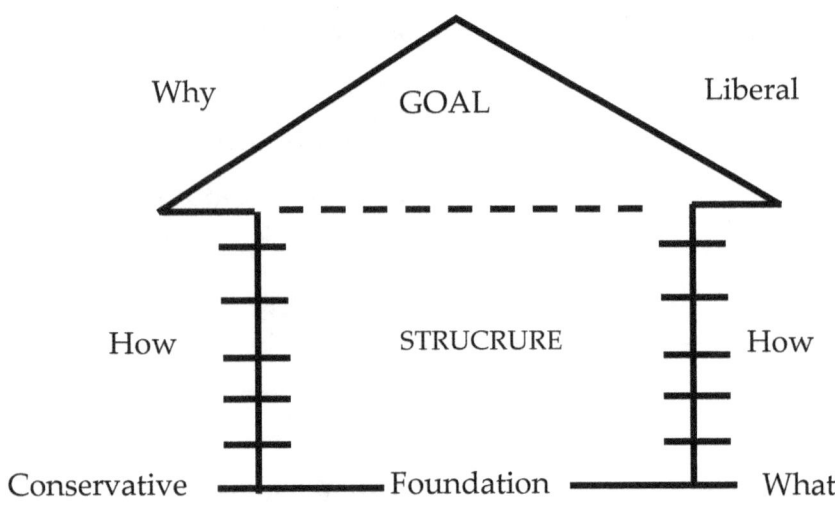

Conservative: The Foundation

Everything that exists in this world is built upon some form of groundwork. Conservatives can often come across as brash and harsh, with little to no empathy. It's the truth hurts and too bad if you can't survive. Heavy in tradition (in most cases) they become set in their way of thinking early on, and as time passes, rarely allow for a change in perspective. It's what is familiar and comfortable to them. It is the way it has always been.

While at times this can seem detrimental, the failing limitation being that it cannot evolve (perhaps not seeing the need to), there are many attributes that can be beneficial, if applied correctly.

1. Grounded in reality. Accepting and open to harsh truths.

2. Strong set of values and moral code.

3. Take and apply things in its simplest form. Free of needless confusion.

Over the entire course of the twentieth century onwards, the foundation in which we have conducted ourselves has slowly become less and less restrictive, with each generation shunning the other for its lack of ethics. For example, the breakdown of the bourgeois class system in the early 1910s evolved towards the various romanticized forms of media to the 1930s and 40s being a complete juxtaposition to the context of depression and war. This separation of family evolved into the distinct husband and wife dynamic of the 1950s, which slowly began to crumble with the introduction of rock n roll, and peaking with the anti-cultural revolution of the 1960s.

With each new generation, we move further and further away from these fixed ideals to a much freer outlook. This is important as too much structure can be suffocating and rigid, however we have to be careful not to lose it to the point where we have no foundation. A house without a strong foundation, will eventually crumble, and when it does, you will be left picking up the pieces wondering where you went wrong. Remember, all thought (and the subsequent results and experience) is based on what it is founded upon. In order to build a strong house, you need a solid foundation. One grounded in reality.

Liberal: The Roof

Next, comes the roof. Odd you may think that we are worrying about the top of the structure, when we haven't even built the rest of the house, however, this reasoning symbolizes something that all higher seeking beings strive for. A goal.

Social justice, women's rights, climate change, equality. They have the end result to strive for. It is the vision. The 'higher purpose'. Now of course it is important to dream, as we need a direction to go towards, but in a world with multiple pathways and agendas, we still need to know **what** we are building and **why** we are building it.

In pursing any goal, be it a small-scale task or a global movement, it is very easy to become lost in it. The further you lose yourself in the glamour of it, the more you lose a grounding to reality. It becomes very easy to gravitate towards the one-dimensional aspects. Often the case with such an outlook, is we have the dream, but no real understanding of how to get there. Think 'easier said than done'.

The Pencil is Mightier Than the Perception

One of my first jobs out of school was working as a labourer's assistant installing fences. For every post there was a hole that needed to be dug by a shovel, then filled with concrete. Depending on the length that was quite a few. Prior to this, I never once thought of all the work that went into the construction of such a structure. The materials. The equipment. The labouring and hours. Sometimes we forget that in our monotonous existence, monumental feats of ingenuity, planning and networking occur for it to be that way.

Economist Milton Friedman, Winner of the 1976 Nobel Memorial Prize in Economic Science, explained it best when referring to a pencil (a homage to the essay titled *I Pencil* by Leonard Read).

"Look at this lead pencil. There's not a single person in the world who could make this pencil. Remarkable statement? Not at all. The wood from which it is made, for all I know, comes from a tree that was cut down in the state of Washington. To cut down that tree, it took a saw. To make the saw, it took steel. To make steel, it

took iron ore. This black centre—we call it lead but it's really graphite, compressed graphite—I'm not sure where it comes from, but I think it comes from some mines in South America. This red top up here, this eraser, a bit of rubber, probably comes from Malaya, where the rubber tree isn't even native! It was imported from South America by some businessmen with the help of the British government. This brass ferrule? I haven't the slightest idea where it came from. Or the yellow paint! Or the paint that made the black lines. Or the glue that holds it together. Literally thousands of people co-operated to make this pencil. People who don't speak the same language, who practice different religions, who might hate one another if they ever met! When you go down to the store and buy this pencil, you are in effect trading a few minutes of your time for a few seconds of the time of all those thousands of people".

This can be applied to any object surrounding you right now. Don't forget the building you are sitting in. The road you drove on to get there. The car you used. This simple observation and awareness put things into real perspective that nothing is made for free, and in the grand scheme of things there has to be an incentive for something to exist. A return of value. Now this of course doesn't exclude this value from being brought about by greed and power, however, if we can conduct our approach in such a way that addresses things practically (starting small), we will find our desired movements develop into having much more traction. Remember, without a structured way to get there, the roof cannot stand, and without a foundation, nothing of longeval value can exist.

The Structure

As the foundation defines **what** we are building, and the roof the **why** we are building it, the structure represents **how** we get there. The steps in between the sequence from start to finish. Ironically, in today's current environment of convenience and immediate-gratification, we either seem to fall towards either what is easier to see in front of us (physically) or far from our reach (mentally).

What we should strive for, (and what I realised myself, is the **appreciation of the process**. Refer back to the cycle of perception. It can also be a used to illustrate the roundabout effect that occurs when two parties from opposing positions and perspectives clash. Consider this;

You hire a team of engineers and builders each specializing in different fields. They argue and bicker that their way is the best in order to build the structure. It feels like hours until a decision is made, but even then, no progress has developed and they only make the decision to stop the squabbling. If only both 'sides' would bring together both their unique set of skills and perspectives to decide the best steps to build the best house, instead of indulging in their ego and the need to be right. It is not who is right, but what is.

To find what is right, we have to compare, contrast and discuss.

The problem is, most discussions almost always end up turning into a debate. This is why any form of debate is, in the large scheme of things, utterly pointless. It serves as a way to prove their point. I am right and you are wrong. Not, how can we use these viewpoints in conjunction, to move towards a solution?

American economist, Thomas Sowell, (who was a protégée and later colleague of Milton Friedman) once stated that; *"There are no solutions, only trade-offs. Whatever you do to deal with one of man's flaws, it creates another problem, but you try to get the best trade-off you can get. That is all you can hope for".*

I agree with his statement. There is indeed no one-step solution for everything. One thing does indeed affect everything. However, in a sort of enlightened way, I believe the two are much closer than first perceived. Rather than seeing the solution as this resolutive factor to dissolve an issue, the 'solution' is the process, the structure. There is a solution there, but to get to it, we must break it down until there are as little trade-offs as possible. Minute in their negative effects. There will always be trade-offs, a cause and effect, but in this instance, to the point where the trade-offs are so miniscule, everything is equal and equitable in their relativity.

Three Sides to The Coin

You may think that, with there being opposite sides to a coin, it is a two-dimensional object. Pick one up and look again. What is holding them together? There is a **third** piece to the puzzle, a common interest that runs along the middle. This is the true key to fully understanding a situation. Not right or wrong, this or that, but simply what **is,** with the common interest being the outcome that favours not a party or opinion, but the bigger picture. The situation that allows the two 'sides' to exist is what the focus should be on. Sometimes you need to put aside your ego and pride aside and see it from the other perspective. (See *Becoming the person you tried not to be*).

The situation may be bigger than you, but you can always be bigger than what your preconceived beliefs are. What is 'right' is not based upon not the ethics you hold by your habitus, but what fundamental principle/morals the situation is founded on. Although an engineer's outlook may be different, their purpose is the same. Build a house that functions. Like the three-dimensional coin, there is a common interest that joins the two perspectives together, working in harmony to provide support to the other in a sequence. In order to strive to be equal, we need to realise that we are different. Equal in, but different in method. The common ideal is the bridging of both.

Note: You may wonder why I did not classify the structure as being centrist or libertarian. At first, yes. I can see why you would make this assumption, however that would defeat the purpose of this chapter. By identifying it as just another viewpoint, it would easily be open for the other to oppose. It is crucial to transcend your belief to realise there is no belief, but 'just is'. Depending on what 'side' you are originating from, we must learn about the other's perspective, show empathy towards their experiences, and consider the limits that your place resides in the overall goal.

Can Peace Exist Without Chaos?

In this current climate where everything seems to be getting exponentially dire, the peace that we so long for seems to be evaporating ever so delicately into the atmosphere. It makes you wonder. Can the source of chaos that is ever present and evolving be stopped? In reference to Greek mythology and Hesiod's *Works and*

Days, consider this question in the form of a metaphor. Can Pandora's box, ever be closed?
It is always open, always there,
but if we keep it hidden, buried deep down amongst the earth,
It will have as much effect as the worms in the grass do
against our decaying corpses. Only when we choose to fertilize its
message with actions of wrath, do we continue to keep its lid open?
Both aware, and unaware of its presence and impact on the wider
world it rests its corners in?
The box is open and closed simultaneously.
For how long? To what extent?
That depends on two things.
Us as humans, and the context in which we existent in,
It stays open as long as we will it to. While the will that keeps it
open stays as long as we allow it.

After writing this poem, I found myself back once more at my grandmother's revolving table, and the small works of poetry that I had known so much about. Like an echo of an otherworldly voice, they called to me (the book I initially picked up was ironically on outer body experiences). I opened the cover to the words, THE COLORS OF LIFE: The International Library of Poetry. I knew straight away upon reading the title alone, that it would fit harmoniously here. When I did eventually reveal to her (by asking for her permission), that I would be utilising her poetry in this book, a sudden warmth came over her.

"Yes of course. Which one"?

HOPE

The mind droned with gloom, cold utterances of pain
Like a silvery moon that waxes but never ever wanes
Entangled in a silky web the grey and misty tears
Emotions devoid of meaning cast to ashes o'er the years

The stars have spent their glittering,
The rays of dawn are near
My life almost ebbed of living
When a glimmer of hope appeared
Challenging my soul, my being, hope let the anger sleep
Building a temple in the heart
While the spirit no longer weeps.

Every moment is precious since hope bewitched its way
Weaving a web of wisdom, hope decided to stay
With clarity of voice its power is commanding
While inner flowers bloom,
Bringing peace and understanding.

Holding hands in the hush of time
A spiritual faith is purling
For hope is my companion now, our destinies unfurling
That sanctuary of faith with courage every day
Nurtured every vision when hope decided to stay.

Sybil Bauer

How To Be Truly Attractive

The law of attraction is a concept that baffles even the most intrepid romantic. If I were to ask you the ratio of you being attracted to someone to them being attracted to you, I'm sure you would reply; "What ratio?". All throughout my early-adolescent years, I was petrified by women. Well, not so much women, more the thought of rejection. What they might say. The aftermath of my failure circulating across the school-yard. That awkward feeling of being a loser. Why is it that so many are able to attract the person of their dreams, while I was here surrounded by a lesser reality?

What Makes Someone Attractive?
As touched on in the chapter detailing the cycle of perception, once I began to evaluate the foundation that my feelings were based upon, I saw exactly how my behaviour actually came across to those I interacted with. The first thing you must realise about attraction is this;

Attraction is like a mirror. You are what you attract.

What do I mean by this? That, if all I am attracting are experiences where I am rejected or with people I am not drawn to, I must be that too? Well, I am not going to say no, but what I can provide is an alternative way of looking at this whole concept.

The Vibe
Ask yourself. What do you find attractive? Confidence. Well, so do they. Like the cycle of perception, attraction falls under the same

principle of understanding how your demeanour and self-image **reflect the way other's see you**. It is a genuine state of being, and is receptive to the energy that you give off.

Your Vibe + Their Vibe = Attraction/Rejection

Most people have no idea what type of energy or 'vibe' they give off. They are so caught up in their desire and thought of what might be, that they come across insecure, creepy and strong (not in a good way). Referring back to the section of dealing with rejection, I now understand what they meant by; "You just come on too strong". Notice that in the equation, things have to be reciprocated. A single positive and a negative cannot equal another positive. One value cannot attract the other by itself. Simply put, people find attractive the attributes that they want to see within themselves.

Alpha Or Beta?

You may have heard the terms Alpha and Beta. These are used to describe the level of confidence that people have in regards to attraction, and the reason for why one is either successful, or unsuccessful in dating. Women want to date alphas, and men what to be them. This of course goes back to our primal instincts, with females looking for males that can act as providers and males looking for females that can bear offspring. Now of course, we should never go into viewing someone with such preconceived ideas, however biological speaking, this has not changed at its core in terms of attraction. It is there, just subtle and subconscious, and therefore it is crucial to know in order to create a persona that can achieve such success. (Refer to *The Dynamic Masculinity & Femininity*).

Alphas, are described as being natural leaders. Decisive. Strong. Calm. Betas, on the other hand, are much more sensitive within themselves. I can tell you from experience we let our emotions run our decisions. We overthink, are indecisive and helplessly needy. Betas, are for the better term, the nice guys/girls. This is typically seen as something directed only for males, but in my observations, I believe this applies to us as a collective. Regardless of gender. Some people are born with attributes that naturally allow them to be classified as an alpha. One-dimensionally, this is most often physical. We are trained to take things at face value, and thus determine looks as being separate to personality. Different people will attract different things, or what is 'in your league' as the term goes. This is true, but as a term, it is just a series of words. What is more important is understanding the reasons behind attracting the people and experiences we do.

There is a key difference between someone that **looks attractive** and **is attractive**.

There are various dynamics that one can use when determining why someone is attractive/unattractive.

1. Looks attractive, but lacks a notable personality, awareness and accountability to their ego. As you might conclude in the chapter (Having *Sex vs. A Sexual Experience)*, superficial people attract superficial things.

2. Looks unattractive, but has a good heart and soul. Needs to work on themselves to a create a positive image. Usually looks for things out of their league or for a better term; **unable to reach**.

3. Looks decent. Has potential but needs to work on one's self by first realizing they have a higher standard.

4. Unattractive and bad personality. This is caused by our past experiences, being treated bad and having a bitterness towards others, and ultimately, oneself.

It is easy to be hostile towards these types of people with their perfect bodies, wealth and success. "It is the only reason these people are successful". Now, take that bitterness away. Why are you really bitter? Jealous because they already have what you wish onto yourself? In some aspects, you are indeed right about these types of people. However, given the nature of things, they will discover that there is much more to being a person than adhering to a type. They will find it will become difficult to regain their sense of identity within these constrictive parameters. Alphas in their arrogance and superficiality, and betas in their sorrow and insecurities.

Rather than having this passive-aggressive approach, I find it more beneficial to approach things from a more **assertive perspective**. When I see someone with such qualities, I ask myself, what strategies can I take and implement for myself? Perhaps it is to learn about fashion. To get in shape. To become more literate. Alpha. Beta. They are just words. Without words, there is just a person left. Being attractive is completely dependent on having totality in one's self. It is an external entity that is perpetuated by how you inwardly see yourself. All your qualities are on display.

So, any form of worry, neediness and insecurity are all negative attributes that are causing you to not attract. The solution, is to take the essence of each type. To create a balanced person. Betas will need to learn how to be more commanding and confident, while alphas will need to learn gentleness, empathy, and compassion.

Changing Your Appearance: Finding Your 'Style'

Now even though, (depending on which one of those four categories you find yourself in), we must conclude that despite their being a difference between looking and being attractive, your appearance still does play a factor. You may come across people while out and thought to yourself; if they just changed their hairstyle or lost some weight, got into shape, or bought some new clothes, they would be deemed acceptable by society's standard of beauty.

You would be right, but to a degree. It depends on how the individual at question interprets this, and specifically where they are coming from. For example, we say to ourselves; "If I buy nice clothes, then that will change things". For some, this may work, temporarily, but for most, all it will do is put a worried man in nice clothes. It doesn't match. Don't try bake a cake, when you don't have all the right ingredients. One measurement wrong by the tiniest amount, will spoil it. Remember the ultimate principles. You can't change your exterior to get satisfying results. To be attractive to others, you must be attractive within yourself. Don't dress to impress. Dress for you. Learn about fashion. What size works for your current body shape. The colours and shades that suit your skin tone. Work with what you have whilst working on your weaknesses. Clothing and style, if used correctly, are a clever way of hiding your flaws. If not, they only accentuate the accumulations of your poor lifestyle. On the opposing end, there are those who misinterpret this knowledge in thinking that looks are all that matters, and thus become one-dimensional in their persona. Yes, appearance is important, not simply to look appealing, but because it is a reflection of how one presents themselves. What does your presentation say about you? That you take care of your appearance? Or that you are too materialistic and shallow? **It's not even what you wear necessarily, but how you wear it. Finding the right balance between trying too hard, and not enough.**

The next time you are struggling to decide what outfit to wear, think of these three things. The seriousness of the situation/event, the weather/setting, and what makes you feel good/showcases your personality. The accumulation of looks, mindset and intention. The truly attractive one is someone who pledges; "I want to make a change for myself, not because of anyone else, but just to improve and grow". This is the most unselfish selfish act one can do. It is also the most honest. It puts you in an extremely vulnerable situation to accept who you are now, to where you have to be. (See *Being Honestly Vulnerable*).

Being In the Moment

From the dull and lifeless view given by my seat's slightly tinted window, I wasn't expecting to see much for the rest of my journey home. Despite having gained control over my vice for about a month, I was still returning from another day of monotonous work for a job I found no solace in. Being late at night, the train was almost empty, so like usual it was another time of me being left alone with my thoughts. With my town's station nearing closer, I got up early and exited the middle of the carriage, in hopes to waste no time when stepping off onto the platform. So, there I was, waiting for the doors to open, when suddenly a young woman appeared. Tall. Fair featured. She certainly looked attractive. With straight auburn hair that fell to her chest, she began attending to it in the reflection of the opposing doorway. Now normally I would be too caught up in my own head thinking about how to start a conversation, hoping she would notice, but this time, without hesitation.

"Don't worry. You look fine". What! What did I just say! Where did that come from? As if an entirely separate entity had possessed me, I spoke these words I thought I would never say. Her eyes looked up at me from her image in the window. She turned her face towards me, brushing her hair back from her cheek. She smiled, blushing. Almost taken off-guard by the comment.

It was at that moment, the doors opened. I could have said something like; "ladies first", but for whatever reason, I resisted the urge. If was I on a mission, not giving off more than I needed to. *

The question how to attract and be attractive, are one of the same. Being truly attractive is not something that is superficial, or viewed as a single entity. It something other-worldly, a space in between things that like a magnet pushes and pulls two forces to one another. It's who they are inside. It radiates from their soul into the space that is attraction. Ultimately, you should not be concerned with attracting, but rather becoming content within ones-self to then allow things to come. This concept will be expanded upon and become clearer in the sections; Love & *Dating Flow and How to*

Read the Situation, yet I feel as the two go in tandem, this can act as a prelude to becoming more aware. With that being said, in regards to attracting someone;

1. You can't go in wanting anything from, or expecting everything out of them.

2. Don't see them as you want to see them (a one-dimensional fantasy). Instead, see them as they present themselves to you. On their merit. This will require a calm mindset free of expectation, (see page 257), and an understanding that this determines when and what kind of things will come into your life circle.

3. **It's the situation that provides and decides if the attraction can occur.** NOT YOU! Your role only arises, when is it necessary to take courage as a final step.

Looking back, I can now recall ample opportunities where the situation had presented itself, yet I had not acted upon it by making a move. However, as you will read in the chapter on page 129, had I taken action, things would have ultimately unfolded the same. Despite showing courage in that moment, things would have never been sustained long-term, as the other parts of myself had not been refined/fully realised.

You have to take it for what it is now, as opposed to what you want it to be.

In the moment philosophy provides the upmost opportunity for the state of attraction to occur. The best and most genuine attractions occur when both people are comfortable within themselves and see things the same way (on the same page). This identical mindset creates a new pathway for that couple to explore through, opening up new challenges that each other haven't experienced and are only available to those in harmony. You will find things will naturally come your way if you are focused on what you are doing genuinely. Not trying to find it. You can't find it. In order to find something, you have to have lost it at some point. If you are not attached to the outcome, you are relaxed, calm and will be truly surprised when something good enters your existence.

*I had already started to venture forth when she joined me on the platform. Unlike times before, I did not wait for her eagerly like a lost puppy, but walked my own path. Not concerned whether she was showing interest. I asked her about her day. What she did for a living. All the usual things one does to spark up a discussion (although there was no grander intention). She then slowed her pace, matching my question with answers. We eventually reached the end of the platform. She turned to go one way, where I turned to go the other. We sat in a symphony of silence as we both realised this was the crossroads of a decision.

"Well, have a goodnight", I instinctively replied, smiling. It was then that we both consciously made the decision to turn and part our separate ways. I admit I may have looked forward to that day the following week, hoping she would take the same train, but alas that day never came to fruition. Do I regret not asking her out? Perhaps. Do I think this moment could all be one-sided my head? Possibly. However, I believe by me only trying to justifying it, only proves its genuine value. It was to give me the reassurance that the work I had done on myself in that past month had been worth it. It was not in vain. I realised it was just bigger than what I required at that time.

Being 'Honestly' Vulnerable

When most people think of being vulnerable, they immediately associate it with negative connotations. Without really thinking, they identify it as a weakness tied directly to emotions. Now to a degree is this true, but what people forget to realise is that there is a strong distinction between feeling bad/having bad thoughts, and being honestly vulnerable. A hard pill to swallow, it takes a full dose a detachment to truly understand its deeper meanings. People tend to hide their fears and insecurities by putting up a wall (remember facades). This wall, if ever attacked, sends out a range of defences; rage/anger, panic and quick decisions. These emotions are expressions of thought. Thoughts that have manifested into feelings that are ultimately expressed through brash behaviour. As a result, you become dependent on people feeling pity for your situation.

Sympathy: Sharing feelings of pity towards another's situation.

Empathy: Understanding why the other's situation brings about these feelings.

Apathy: Feeling indifferent. Lacking emotion or any inherent interest.

The only person who is feeling bad is the one that is just that. The one that feels. You are the one that controls your feelings. This pity does not apply directly to these other people that you wish would feel bad **for** you. No one can read your mind and understand what exactly it is you are going through **unless** they have experienced it themselves. Now if you are vulnerable for example, through a sickness, this is more understandable to people, as most likely they have experienced that themselves. Sympathy may lead to empathy; however, it is far more difficult to reach a state of empathy by itself. You can feel bad for someone just on a surface level. Experiencing empathy towards someone is when you begin understanding their struggles on a deeper level, and able to acknowledge its effect. Being vulnerable in this context actually acts as a way of pushing forth strength of character and heart, as you are doing so in a direct accepting way. There is no need to fear what other may think, as you have no fear of it yourself (See *The Antidote to Fear*). It brings out your inner warrior. We are often taught that it is not very masculine to be vulnerable, and to a degree in certain contexts, it is correct. (Refer to the section on masculinity and femininity). As I began to see the transformation in myself from unsureness and worry, to clear decisiveness, I realised how much the foundation this vulnerability is derived from, plays a part in making an impact. Therefore, there is ultimately, a **difference between being superficially vulnerable, and being purely honest within yourself**. For example, you should not expect people to show you empathy, and certainly don't illustrate this in your demeanour. Sulking around, expecting them to express their sympathy for your situation. For those that have a tough exterior, you must search within yourself, past all the emotion and pride to bring forth what is honest and real to the surface. When you are vulnerable, you are still a part of your true self, a part that has walls of artificial thought and fear. Making that distinct choice to break that down is masculine. Being vulnerable is real. Feeling bad is an illusion. Embrace the vulnerability within yourself, and (when used in the correct context), reap the response from others.

Love & Dating Flow

We are here. The aspect of everyone's life where we always seem to have problems with. Love. We all want it, need it, and at some stage, wish it never existed. It is again, like an in-between force that commands us to a feeling of pure satisfaction, yet also to near self-destruction. Why? The first thing to understand why you aren't successful in this aspect is to realise that love isn't something you can or must understand. It is universal in its form and thus all flowing. Like the equation (page 69), it is linked to a series of uncontrollable intersecting pathways. Constantly opening and closing. One minute it isn't there and the next it suddenly has entered the existence of the consciousness between our subconscious, and we just...know.

But I Already Know I Am Ready

"I'm ready for love", you say. "I know I am". Well, why are you here searching answers for your misfortune?

Most people view love as being the heightened romanticized version you see in movies and literature. Butterflies. Love at first sight. Marriage. Kids. Yes, this will indeed be the feeling that will come across us one day, however, in our quest for love we fail to realise that love isn't something you create, find or look for. It is a force above all things. Love is deep, meaningful, evolving and calm. Love just is. However, although it is something that is already there, we fantasize about having this for the future, rather than what is in our life now, and what needs to happen in order to receive it. THIS is the focus we should be giving to ourselves, by learning to attract what we are able to and need for us in our life NOW. You probably are 'longing for' that special someone (those words are an indication as to why things aren't working), but deep down, ask yourself, are you hoping this will automatically fix all <u>your</u> problems? Even if you are able to attract this, ask yourself if it is simply the gratification of your expectation being filled? If so, this is an illusion. One-dimensional in its form, and thus only has a limited life-span.

What If I Have Been Heartbroken?

Unrequited love. It rips our soul in two. Leaving us to pick up the pieces. A difficult enough task, as the more we try to mend a broken heart, the more we get cut by the jagged edges lined with guilt and despair. This might be confronting to hear, but in a lot of ways, it is possible for you to break your own heart. Through expectation, attachment and a lack of reassurance to yourself. Now of course, there are multiple scenarios where it is directly brought upon by the other person, yet ask yourself, did you contribute to this in any way, at all? This heartache, if looked at without emotion, can be an insight into something you need to change. We need the answers, to understanding why this all happened, yet don't always get them (even when we do it is too painful to comprehend). So, we sit in the sorrow trying to process what turns to self-guilt. Time does heal wounds, but when these wounds are self-inflicted, we need to understand why.

For example, say you have found out your partner has been cheating. The pain will hit you like a tonne of bricks and your immediate response will be hatred for your significant other. You feel less than. Betrayed. However, a bigger lesson can be learnt if one is willing to let their immediate emotions pass.

Look inside yourself to see what you can improve on. Can you learn to be more of an authoritative figure? Can you learn to get in touch with your compassionate or sexual side? Say they do not tell you (you find out through a friend), there can many different avenues that this can exist on.

1. They believed it to be no big deal, as there was no emotional connection to the sex. (To fill a part of themselves that has been lost, or neglected by the partner).

2. They know they should tell you, but are ashamed and are ridden with guilt. They do not want to deal with the coming events that follow.

3. They believe they can just mistreat you and get away with it. Again, there was nothing to it.

Interestingly, all these in some way can intersect one another, and this is where the difficulty lies. How do you know which part is true? By tossing away your emotional attachment to the outcome first, you will then be able to make a clear judgement. You will know if your partner is truly, deeply sorry. The defining factor when they come to cheating is what it is based upon. Mistrust and an upmost disrespect for a partner. If that is the case, the answer (and appropriate response) is clear.

Doubts

The experience (with the excitement and feeling that you ultimately desire) happens only when you are both on the same page. If you are having doubts about a person and what page they are on, the best thing to do is to communicate to them. (Refer to *Being Honestly Vulnerable & How to 'Win' An Argument*). If you have a question, ask it. This being said, the whole 'page' concept indeed makes it difficult. In some cases, we put pressure on ourselves to ask this question, and as a result the answers come from a place of worry, not because we genuinely want to get answers for our betterment. Going back to cheating, you may have doubts about your partner and their potential infidelity. It is extremely vital to not mistake this for doubts within yourself. If they are cheating, or later decide to, it **may** be because of these doubts that only create the context for that cheating to exist.

Either way, the truth will come out. Whether they tell you directly or not. The point is, as long as you are calm, and strong within yourself, it does not matter. Their true colours will be shown. On the opposing side, if you want to end it with your partner, end it. Explain what is going through your head, and more importantly, why it is. Don't cheat. Plain and simple. It creates more problems than it solves through a fleeting moment of 'pleasure'.

How This Applies to Dating

We often equate love with being reserved for only those in a relationship or marriage. While yes, this is a deep meaningful love with a purpose and direction, often the case is that when approaching this aspect of our lives, anything less than the highest level is constricted to a box of labels and types. Casual. Just friends. Friends with benefits. All these are just words, and while they do have merit in terms of defining your appropriate boundary of feelings, what I am specifically referring to is the preconditioned terms and notions surrounding such, that causes overthinking, misunderstanding and disappointment. We go into dating with expectations of a certain feeling or 'spark', and this long list of requirements that if they don't meet up to them or tick every box, then they are no good to us. In their limited form, these terms fail to acknowledge what love is in its most simple level. A mutual understanding and appreciation for another. With these notions already in our head, we repress the natural flow of circumstances that allow the deeper feelings that come with understanding a person. Now, you could argue that these circumstances are natural in that they were going to happen regardless. (See *The Equation & Did I do the Right Thing?*) However, even after things were said and done, I always went away, feeling I could have avoided it all. That, ultimately, there must be a better way to going about things.

It is not that dating is hard. It is that we make dating hard.

You should NEVER go into a relationship thinking "If they just changed this one thing, then things would be perfect". People can change, but you should NEVER try to change them into what you want them to be. These are signs that you haven't yet accepted the love that is within yourself. (See pages 180, 181). Love is three-dimensional; thus, you have to take the good, the bad, and the ugly of someone, and they (if genuine) will do the same for you. Nothing is perfect, no matter how much romanticism lets on for you to believe. I was once asked by a friend what traits I found attractive in a person. What was my type? I replied with the following.

"You can have all these things you find attractive, but that is extremely one dimensional. What is more important is how it ties together to the person and their aura/personality. It has to match. So, what I am saying is although I find certain physical attributes attractive, there can be someone without those things and because of their personality that I'll find them attractive. So, I have a type whilst not having one, or not having one whilst having one".

They key is to not go into dating with an idea of what you want, or what this person can be. Think of them, and treat them as just that; a person. A person with emotions, fears, desires, a past and a reason for why they are here in this current form. Again, when you apply labels without events happening first, you set them up to either succeed or fail on expectations. Let them reveal that themselves to you. Don't force it! You don't decide when to date them, the situation should naturally provide you the opportunity, and you should effortlessly take it. On my last attempt of dating online, someone once told me. "Dating is like a fart, if you force it, it's probably shit". Thanks Emma, you are probably right, but you have to put in a bit of effort to know if it will even come out.

Is Dating Even the Right Word?

When it comes to dates, and dating in general, in most cases we have already put an expectation on where it has to go. This is fine if you both want the same thing in regards to courtship, yet so many people create an unreasonable amount of pressure, especially when you are young and have ambitions around creating yourself and your career. I always looked at it two ways. Either you will eventually marry them, or break up. Now you could say this was merely a reflection of a fear of commitment, but I feel it was based more on the factor of cautiousness. Wanting to be ready at the right time. I knew the path I wanted to go, and was aware a relationship could only complicate things. Why be involved with someone when I knew I could not fully commit. There must be a way that combines something that is free flowing like dating, but without the added pressure or expectations given when courting someone?

I once wrote a full seven step plan, outlining the 'way' to go about courtship, from getting a number all the way to the third 'date'. At first this approach seemed to work, but soon I wasn't achieving the results/feeling I should have. Why? You can't follow a plan to 'date' someone. It becomes too static. It is supposed to be flowing and spontaneous. We seem to be more concerned about the terms than the people that we are out with. Don't identify it as a date or hangout or whatever. Just be, with them. Two human beings, being in the moment. It's all a date and a hangout at the same time whilst being neither of those things. You will find that you will evaluate how the experience went between you two, and naturally will then categorize it on a specific level. Again, the situation provides itself, not you forcing it out of expectations, loneliness or some subconscious way of thinking. The words of spiritual teacher and inspirational speaker, Iyanla Vanzant, made this clear to me.

> *"Look for the **experience**, not the feeling. Look for the **experience**, NOT the excitement."*

"But you said, love isn't something you look for"? Indeed, this is true, but do not confuse this with expecting. The better term would be **ready to receive the experience**. What is meant by experience? As you will discover, I believe it is, in its simplest form, the space. The space between one another that draw you to the present moment. By expecting the feeling and excitement, we have already put an outcome for this person to reach. And when these do not reach that outcome, we have unknowingly set ourselves up for disappointment. Ironically, I found that when I put everything aside and just saw it from a perspective devoid of preconceived notions, I found no longer was I achieving the same results of failure. Rather, receiving a different one altogether.

Be Independent (Bringing Things Back to You)

The more I started to lose attachment to the need for others and move forth with my goal, I found things naturally came my way. Remember, you are in control of what comes into your space. Apart of this is making sure you create a space that puts your life first, whilst one that is not concerned of whether you are with someone. As it will be expanded upon in *the Dynamic: Masculinity vs. Femininity,* having the choice means letting them showcase themselves and see if they hold up to your own self. Set boundaries and standards, but not to the extent they become the reasons for people not being able to pass into the realm of a genuine experience. They say that you shouldn't judge a book by its cover. That first impressions are everything. If both are true, then what part is left <u>for/of</u> you to uncover? You picked up this book after all. Either you worked your way from the outside in, or the inside out.

Love At First Sight? Soul Mates or A Choice?

We have all heard the omnipresent notion that one day we will come across someone that you are destined to be with. As if both our souls are perfect in tandem as lovers. However, with a distain for things that are overly spiritual, there are a great number of those who are adamant such a thing as 'love at first sight', is nothing more than a choice. Often, the question comes up whether one must use their head versus their heart, and while I believe I have always had this deeper feeling that made me hold onto the notion of soul mates; love isn't as always as simple as a spark. We forget that it can arise from different circumstances and in a lot of cases, develops overtime. It is in this context, that using our head, holds reason.

Types of Dynamics Where Love Can Form

1. Two people who are doubtful about themselves. They ultimately bring out each other's inner confidence.

2. One confident. One insecure. This can work like a see-saw effect, where the other allows you to see that part of yourself that was hidden.

3. Two confident people who are at the stage in their life where they are sure of themselves.

You can either see it as the people being two halves, that when together, make a whole, **or** two that automatically make another whole. I feel it is irrelevant. They are one of the same. The more important thing is that the whole is made. Just be careful of the foundation the half or whole is built upon.

The feeling of being with someone often clouds with who that someone is. It is only a successful combination of BOTH that is important.

This means, regardless if you use the word 'dating', you have to **have patience**. Sometimes the chemistry is right there, other times you have to give it time in order for it to develop. Romantic. Sexual. Platonic. The important thing to stress is that there are no labels, no expectations, no intention. Just is. (This is taking place secondary to your own life). Think of it as being everything yet nothing at all times, whatever level and dynamic. It is a three-dimensional inclusion of both perspectives, not one from just your own. The joining of two lives (souls) together.

Listening to my head and heart, I know I have to be at my best before I am to make that whole with another. This means the timing has to be right. You have to be at that point in your life to be able to **let it come to you.** My life circle has to match up to the lifelong commitment I am willing to make. Accepting the sacrifices one must make, when accepting their significant other. I have always had a metaphorical image in my mind of what this meant.

Finally, I had a chance to bring it to fruition.

You Stand

You stand alone in the dark depths of a huge cavern.
In the centre, there is a door.
Stoic and silent.
You do not know how it got there or what lies beyond. All you know that it is your only path ahead.
A great chasm separates you from the door.
It appears to go on for miles. Into the unknown.
There is no possible way to reach it. Another person is needed to make the pathway from your side, appear.
Suddenly a light strikes you from the opposite end of the cave.
The sound of faint footsteps echoes across to you. A figure is standing there. You can't make out their face. It is silhouetted in darkness. You try to yell out to them, but your words don't make it across the cavern.
The pathway on the opposite side rises.
Now the figure notices.
They too activate your pathway. It is now shown.
A guiding force that signifies the end of your journey.
You can now safely walk across the chasm.
Reaching the door, you notice it is translucent. You can see the other person through it. You are taken back by their appearance. It feels inviting. Then, without any reason or real sign, you extend your hand. The other takes a second to process your proposal. Almost as if they too are questioning if this is the right thing for them.

Then, as if they are possessed by the same tenacity and thoughts as you, they reach forth their own hand.
Taking one last look at the path you took to get here; you walk your first steps through the door.
Now a new journey awaits. One with its own set of challenges. One where only those who are in harmony will prosper.

So, the question of soul mates or a choice remains. Or does it? Ironically, with all we have discussed, you must now realise there is no answer left to be ascertained. They are one of the same. A choice is made (to be together), but the force that joins that is done so subconsciously without even knowing you have made one. Remember back to the start of this chapter when you exclaimed that "I know that I'm ready"? It may not be the day you physically meet, perhaps later down the track, but when that day comes you decide to share your life with another; unknowns to you, is your soul communicating to you that the time is right. Your love will just suddenly be. Do you believe that love at first sight exists? No? Well, how can you when it is something that relies on the belief of another?

How can you, when no one else does?

ACT III

A Shift In Perspective
(Intermission)

Halfway through writing this manuscript, I found myself struggling how to go about structuring it. I had all these notes put together, but had no real direction about how to sequence them into a coherent narrative. To gain some clarity, I found myself back at my grandmother's house, and the same table that started me on this journey. I came across a cover that immediately sparked a response from my grandmother.

"Your father has read that one".

He was not the reading type. Certainly not anything to do with this topic. In bright glossy sapphire, the words YOU'LL SEE IT WHEN YOU BELEIVE IT caught my attention. The author, Dr. Wayne W. Dyer.

This book was much wordier than Howard's. On the surface it seemed a great task to pick up and start reading. Flicking through the pages, I noticed that certain lines of text were highlighted; underlined in orange against the worn beige of its backdrop. Surely this was my grandmother making observations. Investigating further, I came across a familiar name. My father's. An arrow directed me to another phrase highlighted in fluorescence.

"When you really and truly know that you create every aspect of your daily life, then will you learn to discontinue disharmony or to discover its message."

The chapter this came under was titled *Thought*, the subheading Thursday. I always hated Thursday. It was that time of the week that signified that was almost the weekend but not quite. Teasing you. Then I remembered the messages I had learnt on my journey. Thursday is just a name. A label used to identify and keep track of time. Without it, it is just another day we experience. The paragraph continued.

"When you no longer need to learn how to deal with disharmony in your life, you will stop creating it, and you will create love and harmony virtually everywhere you turn. Today is your day to keep this uppermost in your consciousness all day long".

This reminded me of my final conclusions on momentum. So, now with a fresh attitude, I picked a section and read, clearing all worry and concerns about how to go about writing, and just did. This brought with it new concepts that added to what I had already learnt rand transcribed. Like the very path I was on, the formulation of this book became directly connected to my personal journey, progressing when I did and vice versa.

So, I went back to the table again, this time delving into more work of Dr. Dyer's, as well as expanding my horizons to other areas of interest. Normally, upon seeing these names of accomplished literates and scholars, my mind would move towards a bias based upon what I had seen or heard in relevant media. Then I remembered the concept of branching awareness. Your awareness should be heightened enough now, where you can pick any section, read through it and understand its message based on your need to grow. Not weighed down by any propositioned view. Actually, listen to what they have to say. Consider things from their perspective, absorb what is relevant, discard what is useless, and then bring upon your own experience. Remember structured perspective. What part of the house are they referring to? What structure can be employed to join the two together? Hopefully, the following will bring about a shift in perspective into realizing that such method.

How to Stop Overthinking

This is a question that I'm sure for most, if not all who have picked up this book, is swimming around in their conscious. I can tell you from firsthand experience, the feeling of being in one's head can be at times enraging. Your mind is constantly working, being bombarded with inner thoughts, to the extent that any effort to cease the silence, only makes it more prevalent. When distressed or anxious, the often-used response for someone is to frantically search his/her mind for the answer. "Which way will this go if I take this action? What will be the outcome?".

For myself, I know this originated from my prematurity. The eagerness to get to the outcome before it could even exist. Just like the roof in structured perspective, I already had the ending in sight without knowing the path needed to get there. I innocently (and naively) hoped everything would work out perfectly, simply because I could see it going that way. However, when it eventually (and inevitably) didn't, the foundation that held everything in my existence together, crumbled. In his book, Dyer's covers six aspects associated with an individual's personal liberation.

Thought   Abundance   Oneness   Detachment
Synchronicity   Forgiveness

Upon reading, I immediately drew comparisons to my own observations and experiences, realizing that this would be a prodigious opportunity to showcase my completed ideas and evaluations. The following section expands my own concepts in tandem with Dr. Dyer's outlines as framework, which I believe are in themselves interchangeable. As we have already addressed aspects of forgiveness in the earlier chapters, I will be covering the first five. However, ultimately, they can all be used collectively in a process to address overthinking in its entirety.

Thought

Dr. Wayne W. Dyer's annotations on this highlight the root problem to why we overthink. As he beautifully puts it;

"Whatever you focus your thoughts on expands".

When we tend to overthink, these thoughts are usually negative. Too focused on the future and not enough on the present. Notably when we stay present within our current situation, it is never for what we have but rather what we lack. There examples are all around you in your present lives. Scarcity being for what you don't have. Where you are not at. The job you long for. The relationship you desire. It just becomes all too overwhelming.

You are not any more overwhelmed with the situation as you are with yourself. The ability to not process, address and react accordingly is what instils your anxiety.

What if these thoughts are already expanded? That by trying to discard them, we only give them power. It is much like dealing with addiction. You offset these negative thoughts with another one that disproves its ability to exist. In order to do that, we must first accept them.

That's right. Accept. It is when you acknowledge that which is within yourself, you realise they are nothing more than that. Simply apart of yourself. Thoughts are just that. Thoughts. (Refer back to page 51). We hold control over how much power they hold over us. They come and within an instant and only wish to stay as long as we let them. Unknowingly or willingly.

While Dyer only stated the reasons for overthinking, he also ironically, simultaneously provided the solution. Ultimately, we determine whether or not, they exist.

How To Make Decisions/Let The Outcome Appear

Whether it was contacting a person, going out, or choosing what clothes to wear, I would always hesitate in making a decision. Not only would I become increasingly frustrated with the situation, but would eventually let my emotions drive the way I reacted, and subsequently acted. Even after I awoke from the aftermath of my breakdown, I would remain in a mood for the rest of the afternoon, and in most cases, would resort to my vices. Vices that only reinforced my state.

Sometimes a situation can become quite overwhelming with your mind shuffling itself, overthinking every possible scenario. What might be if you make this certain decision and take this course of action and so on. Not only can it be extremely taxing to your mind, but also to your sense of self. All your time is spent caught up in the 'what if's' instead of the 'what is', to the point where you are no longer able to think rationally and act free of emotion. You must realise by unknowingly suffocating our subconscious mind with conscious thoughts, you only reinstate the negative power your false self has over you! Surely there must be a better way?

Now when I'm talking about decision making, I'm not just referring to simple items such as shoes, food or movies. What I'm alluding to is a much larger choice. The decision that comes with making a choice.

Remember, it is not the situation that we are upset or angry with, it is our ability to control it. The one thing you can control is how you choose to react towards it. You know the best thing you can do when faced with a seemingly unsolvable decision?

"Do nothing".

"What?" You cry. "Nothing at all?"

"Yes".

To be overwhelmed with a decision is to be attached to the outcome. By doing nothing, we immediately eliminate all opportunities for any potential actions to be driven by our emotions. By doing nothing, we simply let nature take its course. Any time I was faced with an anxious thought or noticed I was on the verge of becoming overwhelmed with myself, I immediately abolished it from my mind.

Don't think. Feel. (See *Emotional Content* & How to Read the Situation). If you know deep down it's right, then it probably is. For example, say you are always worrying about the right way to text someone, worried about whether it will make or break the relationship. Simply detach yourself from it. Do nothing. With time, and repetition, soon will you come to the realisation that there is no decision to be made. As there is no longer a problem attached to it. Just another situation that comes immediately and goes an instant later. I can recall a moment where I was becoming increasingly bored, overwhelmed and angry at the same time. With nothing else to do, I sat down, closed my eyes, and went to sleep. I found my body's natural response was to put these thoughts to bed with it.

Although these approaches may appear different, the outcome is fundamentally the same. Depending on your starting point, you can either use this principle of thought to expand on what you already have, no matter how small, and decrease the worry on what you don't. No matter how vast.

Abundance:
What to Do When You Feel You Are Not Good Enough?

If you were to look back at old photos of you in your youth, immediately feelings of embarrassment will flow to the surface. Perhaps, in an effort to stay far away from that as possible, you abolish it from your existence, ashamed of who you were, and are. If this is the case, and I am sure it will be, I implore you to look again.

A reformed perspective will appear. As Dr. Dyer states on abundance;

"Our ability to enjoy life comes from how we choose to process it, rather than from externals. If you need more in order to feel complete, then you will still feel incomplete when you have acquired more".

Crucial in answering this question of feeling inadequate, I believe abundance runs much deeper to our thoughts than any other. In some cases, it can be minute feelings that cause disruptions during the day, while in others, it can lead to dire irreversible consequences to your life. Remember; All pain is relative in the mind of the individual. The same applies here. That person is still you. It will always be. The essence that is you can never change. It is the **context surrounding you** in that particular set of time that is unrealised. You may think because you were not fully understood that this doesn't justify approval, yet I urge you to consider if it had not been for you in that state, you would not only have gotten to this point. You are all those at once. The good, the bad, and the ugly. All that was different was the context that brought it out of you. You knew no better at that period in time. You weren't your true-self.

I remember back to the time most where these feelings were most prevalent. I was out of work, had no social life (constantly rejected by those I met), and had no seeable prospects to look forward to. My only constant was that I was enrolled under a job agency, where advisors would sit down and openly discuss strategies one might undertake to improve employment chances. Perfect, you may think.

Just what you need. Well, if you call me sitting there each hour waiting for my next appointment to be scheduled, then yes, it was exactly what I needed. A catalyst to question. At the end of each session, they handed me a survey to complete, and every time I would fill it out with the same response. To focus more on self-esteem building tasks and individual guidance. These people needed more than a job. They needed confidence. An alternative way of looking at themselves. One particular meeting, instead of the survey, I was given a stapled booklet, each page filled with short answer responses. These questions asked me to write down my favourite qualities about myself and things I needed to improve on. It seemed my persistence paid off. We all know these things about ourselves, yet only when asked, do we truly ask ourselves. It is like your conscious whispering to you over your shoulder; no hesitation and filled with complete honesty. This is your deep feelings coming to the surface.

I am not going to ask you to write down your qualities or things you need to improve on, for I know you already know the answers (but you can if that helps). You possess everything internally that you need to succeed. Reassure yourself this on a daily basis. Any interests you have, you can ultimately do. It may take time, but you can still technically do them. Even if you aren't at that level yet, act as if it is fully realised through you being a work in progress. Your job is to work on filling in those gaps where you need to improve. Use this belief and newfound persona to remind yourself we have everything we need inside of us; it just needs to be unearthed. If we believe nothing is there in the first place, we won't dig.

"It's not what is available or unavailable that determines your level of success and happiness, it is what you convince yourself is true." – Wayne Dyer

Sometimes we feel we can't go on another day. That, if we end it, our troubles within that moment (and ourselves) will cease to exist. Often, we bottle it up, allowing thoughts of self-harm to fester over the course of hours. However, in our urge to supress, we forget there is another way. The air trapped in our subconscious can be let out at any time. We can provide the initial solution to making it to the end of a larger one. Yell it out. At the top of your lungs. Whatever is at the forefront of the mind. I guarantee you will feel an immediate release. As if you have expelled all tension trapped. If you feel you can't make it to the end of the week, month, or year, just make it to the end of the hour. Bring things back to what is directly in front of you (see page 125). Soon that hour will become the day. That's the beauty of it. All troubles that are within you will go to rest, and a new you will emerge with the dawning of the sunrise.

Oneness

Whenever it became apparent that I was showing signs of incompetence, laziness, or lacking course or direction, my father would repeatedly remind me of the following. "Do nothing. Be nothing". Yes, I was lacking direction and being lazy, but despite taking a mental raincheck to these apparent words of wisdom, I was unknowns to him, (and myself), conducting within the parameters of a concept, that I later came to discover as oneness.

Although this may be more attuned to feeling you are not good enough, even in situations where you are affirmative in your actions, there is still that lingering doubt created by outside sources. With circumstances where deep down, I knew I did nothing, yet had pre-emptively convinced myself otherwise. Understanding your thinking and approach behind an issue will help in addressing them in a stress-free, all-encompassing way. **Shaping the outcome by letting it shape around you.** Not letting the outcome, shape you.

How to do this?

Be The Better Man/Woman

Being the better man is a term you have before. It some cases it is a cliché. Giving it a practical application will allow you to calmy approach any situation and problem that is in your self-conscious. Anytime your mind starts to think worryingly, simply ask yourself; "Okay, if I were my true; i.e.; the better man/woman, how would I approach this? What would the better **man** do?" Well, depending on the context. This may be to;

- Open up honestly

- Lose attachment

- Apologize

- Listen

- Sacrifice what is pleasurable

- Show patience

- Show understanding (consider the other perspective)

Now, when I use this word, this does not mean that you are 'better' than others. It simply illustrates how one can implement higher thinking to ultimately create assertive action, as opposed to being aggressive or passive. Sometimes, you may have to show patience, or on the flip side, the situation may require you to confront it (this became especially defusing rumours or misunderstandings). The principle at practice is that everything you do is in your best interest, guided by your best self. Naturally, it will attract the best (true) personality from those around you, and even if it doesn't, it won't bother you. Your true self wouldn't worry or expect things concerning others.

My father would also always say to me; "Stop making excuses". At first, I would only interpret this through his tone as him being stern and unremorseful, however, after coming into my own as someone with higher awareness, I now realise he was only saying this because deep down, he only wanted to best for me. To act on that higher level, is to have no excuses. I good piece of advice always consider your parents advice, as they have been there in your position before. Not this doesn't mean you have to take it, but at the very least evaluate why it is they are saying it in the first place? This advice goes for parents too. As you have been in your child's position before, you should have a level of empathy to understand what it is they are going through and approach their problem in a relating manner. We often struggle to decide whether there is a difference between what we do defining who we are, and who we are defining what we do. There is. The difference is intention. What is that intention based upon?

Hopefully, your better self.

The Time Is Now

Dan Millman, author of the acclaimed novel, *Way of the Peaceful Warrior*, refers to a wise old mentor (whom he called Socrates). At one stage in the book, Dan is asked by Socrates where he was. After the initial back and forth of replying, Dan resorted to "I am on Earth, in the Solar System, in the Universe".

"Where is the universe?"

As Millman expressed, "We ultimately don't know anything. We have gathered beliefs, opinions and facts, but this world still is a mystery". Socrates then asked Dan what time it was, who naturally looked at the clock on the wall.

"The time is here; the place is now.
You are this moment."

I once had a similar moment with a university lecturer, whose lessons I only truly understood after I saw the heightened results of my self-transformation. Towards the end of term, I performed a simple yet poorly constructed speech on law and ethics in the media. Afterwards my tutor, who actually kind resembled the description of Socrates from Millman's novel, asked me whether I had trouble stringing sentences together. "Yes", I replied, recounting events of prematurity and seeing the outcome before it has happened. "When reading", he remarked. "Do you lightly scan as opposed to retain?"

"Yes", I said. He then asked me a question.

"See that door there", he said. "Describe to me step by step how you get from outside this room to where you are sitting".

My first instinct was to blurt out the answer. "You just walk in", however I took a breath, felt the space, and calmly replied.

"Well, I'd extend my hand and turn the doorknob", I said. "Then I'd open the door and walk to my seat, pulling it out to sit down". "Interesting", he replied. "Most people would just walk through the door".

Remember when I referred to not putting off what you could do today? This relates directly to thoughts and overthinking. Whenever you start thinking about the future, to the point where it becomes detrimental, remind you of where you are right at this moment. You are where you need to be exactly now, in order for you to go where you need to be. Even though every aspect of you, past and present, is uniquely yours, in this moment you must see yourself as in the process of being more. Like a sculptor, you have to chip away and mould your material into the artwork that reflects the best of you. I believe we can value where we have come from, and do what is necessary where we are now, in order to go to where we need to be. Yes, this has been repeated profusely throughout, but I believe it opens up a deeper concept that relates to forward thinking.

Detachment

We as children are so innocent without a care in the world. We see things as bright and colourful as they can be. As we grow older, our sense of reality shifts and our responsibilities are broadened. We worry about others and ourselves, losing that sense of childlike wonder and spark for life that we so need as humans.

Just like Dyer highlights, the art of detachment is one of the most powerful tools you can utilise to reattain this aura and resolve self-defeating thoughts. Thoughts attributed to;

- Material items: Clothes, furniture and money.
- Other people: Relationships and 'dating'.
- The need to be right: Our opinion, ideas.
- The past: Events, guilt and revenge.
- Attachment to form: Body, age and technique.
- Attachment to winning and achieving a goal.

Whether your focus is on one or a multitude of these, you still need to understand, that in trying make things easier for yourself, you are ultimately trying too hard. (See page 153).

How to Handle Ageing: The 'Fear' of Getting Older

You notice how on any reality show, when judges address each contestant, they immediately start by asking their age? It is a way of making a series of judgments based on a number. There are people who might hear the comment about how they look the same as when they were younger. "Oh, it's like they don't' age". They do, obviously. It's just their outlook towards it has not. What takes precedent above everything is themselves. When our body starts to wear down, our joints seize up, and skin loosens, we get consumed by this fact, and thus our actions are subconsciously based upon this seemingly dire situation. Yes, you age, but just because you do, it doesn't mean you have to lose that part of you that stops living. Remember, time numerically speaking, is a human construct. Without a means of recording it, it just becomes another day, come and gone as quick as the last. Don't focus on the numbers to the extent where you lose the experience.

See the numbers of years rather than a clock ticking down, a ladder of levels in accumulating skills, knowledge and wisdom.

I still see glimpses of that child-like vibrance glowing out of me as an adult, just it now is reserved for the most special occasions. It is these internal moments that hold together the more external restrictions of your lifestyle. Go to the gym. Keep healthy. (See *Physical Health: Mental Awareness to Transform your Outer Image*). Your body will thank you in the long run. Present yourself well. Those who surprise people with their age don't dress, act or behave based upon what society's standards are for them. Older people can take up fitness (on what level is comfortable), as a means to maintain or cure body aliments, that would otherwise instil a self-defeating philosophy. They don't have to give into the stereotypes that that once you hit a certain age, you need to slow down and drop responsibility. Fearful of the changing world. Now of course this doesn't mean to lose your level of maturity. Rather, lose the inhibition that you are not as invincible as once thought. Noticeable ageing happens is when we take that immaturity and lack of unawareness into adulthood, where it invertedly overrules our growing responsibility. There are consequences to what you do, but with maturing comes the wisdom of knowing the control you hold over what comes into and out of your influence. So, the next time someone asks you how old you are in a way that is designed to make a conclusion of judgement, simply reply;

"How old should I be?

Did I Do The Right Thing?

It was the start of my final year at college. The previous three had been nothing short of lacklustre and uneventful. With the desire to feel less alone growing exponentially, I decided (or more or less hoped) that things this time would be better. On a lunchbreak in-between my classes, I sat in the outskirts of an empty courtyard. Not expecting to meet or converse with anyone, my vision was suddenly struck by a girl who had just sat down at a table nearby. With long black hair that fell down to her shapely torso, she had a presence that I was immediately drawn to. Now normally, I would have overthought it, too fearful of rejection, however this was not the school-yard anymore. The situation presented itself. Affirmative in my action, I walked over to her, asking if the seat was taken. She brought her gaze up to mine, revealing her porcelain skin and sultry smoky eyes. "No", she replied. Smiling.

Meeting with her over the next couple weeks, I noted that despite being very open and lively, she was quite brash and opinionated in her outlook on things.

One afternoon we decided to accompany one another on the train ride home. Despite it being late afternoon, the carriage we sat in was almost empty. On the side closest to the window, I was naturally nervous by the whole scenario. She wasn't. Leaning close, she pressed her hips against me.

My eyes darted from her thighs, to her hands which were now resting on my chest), then lastly her warm glazed lips. With that, we moved in. I received my first kiss.

A day later, I told her that I enjoyed her company on the train, and how the way the kiss made me feel. I then asked her how she felt about it, only to hear a response that would shift everything.

"I do that with all my friends".

That was the last she spoke to me out of choice. I did coincidently come across her a few more times over the year, however despite me greeting her with the same calm and cheerfulness as when we first met, it was clear she still held the same feelings of awkward distaste as her rejection. I ultimately confronted her about the situation, saying I could accept it, but at the very least, I wanted to know why?

"You assumed", she said. "I thought we were just going to have sex".

She was right, I did assume, but so did she. I never even recall talking about that with her. It wasn't even on my mind. I was too busy enjoying each moment. Perhaps that was the problem. *See

The Equation: An Alternative Perspective

This whole event left me with a severe compliancy for settling with anything less than the right dynamic. (See Having *Sex vs. A Sexual Experience*). From the years outside of college, this element I so desired appeared non-existent, no matter who I met, or what I did. I played the event back in my mind, wondering what the outcome would have been if I had taken another form of action. Would things be different? Would I now be in a better place than I am now? What did I do wrong? I came to the realisation, it did not matter what specific action I would have taken, regardless of the order, I would have still been left stranded at the crossroads. The event would have occurred and the outcome would have still been the same. I would have ended up at this exact place. Upset wondering what went wrong, and ultimately forming more mistrust towards my already fragile sense of self. Upon discovering this, I reworked the equation from earlier, to make another.

$$You + time + other$$

$$a+b=C \text{ or } C=a+b$$

$$a+b=C=a+b=C=a+b=C=a+b=C \text{ etc}$$

Looking back at the time equation, you can only control your part. It would not have mattered as to what variable came first, as both the goal and the variables coexist together regardless of what sequence we put it in. The outcome is there, and the moment has the potential to get there, but ask yourself what series of events have to occur in order for that to happen? It is an intricate equation that is far too complex to comprehend when we spend our time stressing over. If I do this, then this will happen, which will cause them to react by doing the following.

In other words, things were ultimately always meant to end up that way. Call it destiny, God's plan, or by looking at it through the equation, your concern as the individual, is identifying your own influence in it, and understanding how it shaped the events to which direction it begins, and continues. The more your perspective grows, the more your knowledge towards yourself does.

Note: (=) Point at which you influence to break the cycle.

As we know from previous chapters, we cannot control how things go when other people are involved. Only what we can. So, having this in mind, our worry is no more self-guilt than it is self-pity. If you influenced it negatively, perhaps by an adverse thought, understand this was your false self at work, and either way, things were simply not able to be. You want to reach the point, where you know you did all you could have, and went about things calmly and without worry. Peace will come across you knowing, you are no bigger than the situation, but the situation is no bigger than you make it. Often when we judge someone it is because we have these levels or standards to live up to and when we get a glimpse of anything that challenges that or falls short, we erect walls of caution to protect ourselves. **The idea is to come to the realisation that it didn't work because it couldn't, rather than because <u>you</u> got in the way.** Now this equation doesn't have to be just used for situations involving people, rather any kind of event that results in you being attached to multiple variables. I have often wondered over the years what it would be like if I had won sporting matches or awards. Sure, there would have been some feelings of accomplishment, but then faster than the moment passed, it was onto the next season.

*A few days later, I rendezvoused with another girl whom I had met a few weeks after initially meeting the first (before the kiss). She invited me back to her apartment on campus (or perhaps I suggested it and she agreed). After we settled in and got comfortable, we started to become 'acquainted', with me initiating the kiss. Although nothing truly physical happened (we could both see it was being forcing), a sense of guilt followed me after. "That was my first kiss", she had exclaimed. Had I deprived her of the feelings I had the pleasure of experiencing? Had I just been to her like that girl was to me? Would she go on to have the same feelings?

A first she did, (we later reconciled), but it brought up an interesting set of thoughts.

Just because chronologically, it may be 'the first', it may not be the first in regards to the genuine experience.

While you could say it was genuine in that it came together by a series of uncoerced events, go further by asking what part of yourself brought it together? To resolve any social issue between opposing sides, we must first acknowledge our influence in the matter. Even if it is something you are deep down ashamed of. Always be accepting of the consequences. By consequences, the continuity that your influence has outside the situation.

"Not everything that is faced can be changed. But nothing can be changed until it is faced"- James Baldwin
If you can show the will to address it, then you are shown true value of what it means to be a man/wo**man**.

Path of Least Resistance

Synchronicity

This passage was once intended to be expanded on it to resemble a chapter like the rest. However, on closer inspection, I realised it would be much better in its form, to drift freely in harmony.

Like a river, the current must flow uninterrupted. Too many obstacles and twists and turns, it turns stale.

Try too hard on something and you are ultimately depriving the truth and process to unravel.

Take things on the level at which they come. Be satisfied with that.

Just relax and let it present itself. Don't force things. Otherwise, it won't be natural, and so won't you in satisfaction.

Branch out your awareness.

It can be hard to do as we see potential in that opportunity or person, but remember to put things first. Bring things back to you.

We stress too much on the issue and this is what is creating the problem.

You create the context in which the problem can exist.

Don't confuse caring for something, with caring for what it represents.

Care by not caring. Having no attachment to its outcome.

We exhaust ourselves trying to succeed, when we don't need to. Don't try, Do. Or do not. We should just do, without hesitation.

The Process. Not the goal.

Meditating
(i.e., The Art of Proper Breathing)

You may roll your eyes when you hear the words 'meditate' or 'yoga'. All that preachy spiritual nonsense. There is no place for it in my life, nor is it something I ever thought of doing. This was exactly my philosophy when it came to the practice. Whenever I attempted to sit down and decide; "Right, I'm going to give this a go", I was always disrupted by the knowledge I was actively trying to calm my mind. I could never reach the desired result of pure relaxation and calm I was promised by the spiritual reputation this exercise held, and as a result I dismissed it.

You may have this preconceived notion of meditating being something only reserved for the divine or enlightened. However, if you have learned anything, the higher thinker will not go into an immediate judgement about things.

Only until realisation through experience, should an opinion be made. Therefore, I implore you to investigate further not into the term, but the content behind it. If you are to take anything out of this word, be it the importance of breathing properly.

The Breath of A Balloon

Originally, the first part of this section was going to bridge the connection between our breathing and the human chakra system. After much deliberation, I concluded that what was listed over a few pages, could be summarised in only a paragraph. Yes, the chakra system is an effective way of illustrating how we can form a deeper understanding of your body (parts of which I will refer to in later sections), but I feel the majority who are already coming into something as uncommon as meditation, will then find it even more difficult to connect. Therefore, before researching anything else, simply do the following.

<u>1.</u> Take a deep breath through your stomach. Like a balloon, let it fill out with air. Most people when they breathe, do it from their chest, using only the top half of their body. Ironically, despite the intention of relieving some of the stress accumulated in our immediate conscious, when done this way, we only trap the negative vibrations even more. Just like hot air rises, so does bad energy, and without allowing your lower half to dissipate that tension, your stress levels only increase.

<u>2.</u> Now, as if you have pulled the ends of the balloon apart, let that breath out by blowing through your lips. Do you feel your whole form becoming much lighter and free? Almost as if you are nothing? Weightless? This is your body expelling all that condensed emotion from such a confined space. Just as one thing affects everything, (and outlined in the chakra system), all sections are like a train track. If one part of the line is blocked, the locomotive that your breath, your lifeforce (or fire) to the engine is easily derailed. Like the operator of the release valve, imagine pushing your breath down and out your body with each exhale. Release that useless vapor into the atmosphere. Take a breath, imagine it filling the affected parts of your body, then release it all with the exhale.

After repeating this method consistently over a period of four weeks, I soon discovered how much of this relates to processing thought. Whenever you feel thoughts of the harmful and undesirable coming back to you, using corrective breathing is vital. It is like a switch that immediately shuts down all negative emotions and thoughts associated with the false self. It resets your being to a complete neutral centre.

I don't know about you, but being the day dreamer (and over thinker) that I was and in part still am, I used to on occasion, imagine scenarios, or 'dream like' fantasies that could happen if I were acting through my true self. Now, I know on countless occasion I have stressed the importance of separating fantasy and reality, but in regards to distinguishing truth from illusion, daydreaming circumstances like these can actually be beneficial. What do you have to be, and what variables have to be in place in order for it to exist? Cycle through all possible elements, intentions, causes and effects, till you reach the point where nothing else disproves or contradicts the outcome. (See pages 255 & 256). You can also relive past experiences, ridden with guilt or unanswered questions, through a sense of understanding and peace. It puts aside all your doubts, and reveals the truth. A truth where only the calmest of minds flourish.

Active Meditation

Sometimes you will find, no matter how hard you try, you just aren't feeling traditional meditation will serve its purpose. The extent of thoughts that are circulating your mind becomes too powerful, to the point where you need a release that doesn't involve going back to destructive habits. A solution that I know from experience proves effective, is a term that involves movement. Active meditation involves having a lively conversation with your thoughts, through a practice that engages your entire body. Be it walking, boxing, weightlifting or yoga to express your emotion through movement, just being able to process your thoughts over and over satisfies the ever-hungry entity that is your mind. The trick is while you are doing an activity that is constructive. I found whenever I became inviting of this uneasiness, combining it with some form of prolongated movement aided in becoming content in my own space. They would, like discussed in the chapter on thought, come and go in an instant. The next time you eat an apple, notice how no matter how hard you try, you can't rush eating it? This is nature's solution for sitting with your thoughts.

By learning to breathe effectively, you will come to the realisation that your body is connected, and having these blockages (physical and mental) are ultimately detrimental to your overall well-being and proclivity. Remember, one thing affects everything. We live in a world now where instant gratification rules supreme, and we think things easily obtained hold the highest value. We are doing things backwards. I now know through meditating, that things are far more satisfying if we earn them through patience and hard work. True satisfaction. By understanding everything grows from the base within yourself, we can take this very model, and use it not only for your life, but others we might come across.

Morning Routine

Remember way back in the first act when I talked about the most common form of self-help? Well, this is an extension of that. Getting into the habit of a strong morning routine is providing the right foundation from which everything else during your day stems from. All the actions you do during this period will reinforce the mindset that will take charge for what is to follow.

I Have Trouble Falling to Sleep

Despite the initial belief of that our problems implementing a consistent routine revolve around what time we wake up in the morning, ironically, it all actually begins the night before. We have all been guilty of sitting on my couch watching television, or looking at a computer screen, watching the hours go by. Many these wasted hours could be reserved for gaining valuable recovery time. "Well, how much do I need"? Six to nine hours is the key they say, yet what they forget to mention, and what is more important than how many hours you get, is what is referred to as deep sleep. This is the period is which your mind is in a full state of rest. The important thing is to remember that time is irrelevant give or take a few hours. You are asleep.

What stops us from achieving this state? The thing that stops all progress. Irrelevant noise. If you are continually concerned and cluttered with excessive thoughts, it will make it extremely difficult to achieve this state of deep sleep. Your body wants to rest, yet your clouded conscious won't let it! Having a rational, dormant mind to begin with will allow you to drift off into nothingness. It isn't concerned with what happened that day or what will become of tomorrow. It is content where it is at in the moment of total slumber.

The 4-4-4 Count

As discussed in the previous chapter, learning the art of proper breathing is an effective way of distilling nagging thoughts. If you cannot achieve this state, and find you are lying there, eyes closed, but mind awake, a technique known as the 4-4-4, will assist you.

1. Breath in slowly and deeply through your diaphragm. Your stomach should expand, <u>not</u> your chest. Count to four.

2. Hold this breath for a count of four.

3. Exhale slowly, blowing out through your mouth for four seconds.

Repeat this process up to three to four times (changing the duration of each count to suit). With each passing cycle, you should slowly feel your body shutting down, with your eyes closing. The fourth time around, your body should be at a state of pure looseness and your mind at total ease.

You can also try wearing a sleeping mask. This will block out any remaining light in your room and help relax your eyes. Also, be aware of the position you are sleeping in. A side on position is the most effective posture wise. For those who are chronic snorer's, sleeping on the back puts your tongue up against the roof of your mouth only to block air flow. Never sleep on your stomach! Not only does it mess up your lower back, hips and rounds your shoulders. It also causes your neck to compress inward. Invest in a therapeutic pillow (and put it between your knees) if you are having trouble transitioning into the side position. Remember when I questioned whether there was something more productive, I could be doing with my time? Try doing some 'mediation', or stretches before jumping into bed.

I Find It Hard to Wake Up in The Morning

Get into the habit of waking up early. I know the luxury of sleeping in is tempting, and sometimes we truly need it, but with our morning state often a reflection of our activity the night prior; it is clear sign we need to disrupt this pattern of conditioning. For example, when your alarm is positioned right next to you, it is easy to hit snooze and fall back into a state of deep inactivity. By setting it far outside your reach, it forces you to get out of bed, and as a result, already moving. From here, this is where your day starts.

I usually follow this by some form of quick movement. Be it push-ups, jumping jacks, arms swings, knee lifts, squats, even walking on the spot. This pumps blood throughout your vascular system, acting like a jump start to shake away any remnants of fatigue. Most people rely on tea or coffee. Don't use this as an excuse to have poor night's sleep. The more you become consistent in following a sleep routine, the more you will slowly lose the reliance for these stimulants. Every now and again is okay though. Drink some water soon after waking up. Your body needs to be hydrated. Also wash your face or have a quick shower, do your hair, and then put on a new-shirt. As if your old one holds all your mental odour from the night before, I always feel fresh after putting on this new suit of armour.

Wake up with the orange haze of a morning sunrise. It symbolizes you are ready to receive everything during that day on its merit.

Making Your Bed

For years, I would be one those people who looked back at the utter mess of intertwined bedsheets and crumpled pillows, thinking; "Yeah, that looks fine". As diminutive as this sounds, making your bed is a representation of the mindset that you will put forth in the 'world' that day. A world that is reactive to the attitudes you hold yourself by. By having a mind that is disciplined, organised and presentable, you are already reaffirming that you would be able to control what may come your way. A cluttered space reflects a cluttered mind. A disjointed bed, reflects a neglect for assertive action. At first, I wasn't making my bed purely out of laziness, thinking, it's just a bed, it does not matter. "Well, if it does not matter, then it should be no problem to fix it?" Once I saw it this way, I could not go without keeping it in order. It felt unnatural to.

Breakfast

Out of the amount of people I talk to, ninety percent of them tell me they have no breakfast. Stimulating conversation, I know. Although they are quite capable of preparing it, they tell me they simply have no time. Regardless of how much time you have in the morning, a substantial breakfast is a must have! If you are travelling, or even having a late tea break, you need something between that time to provide fuel for your decision-making skills.

We see breakfast like it's some mindless activity. I saw it as a way, of becoming competent in handling a hot-stove and pan. The amount of people that don't know how to boil, scramble or fry an egg is astounding.

Stretching

Just like meditation, when we first hear the term 'yoga' or stretching, often our instinct is to dismiss the benefits. Like you are perhaps now thinking, this is either because you associate it with being over-glossy, or because you have no time, or little understanding of your body. Similar to making your bed as means to organise, stretching (or warming up) falls in line with the initial function to energize the body for the day. A means for your body to loosen up and eject any feelings of stiffness from your mind, whilst creating a strong mind-muscle connection. Start simple. Pick one or two exercises for each session, then increase the number of body parts. Most people are weak in these three areas.

Upper-back. Hips. Abdominals.

These three body parts alone provide support to other areas, with a weakness in these are naturally the cause of stiffness in other areas. It works like one long chain.

The upper back, specifically the lower trapezius muscles (centre of shoulder blades), act as the centre for all its surrounding muscles. If you have neck pain, rounding of the shoulders and caving in of the chest, it is probably due to a weakness here.

The hips on the other hand, support the lower half of your base. Our body is predominately used to one of two positions, sitting. Think about it. We wake up, only to sit down at the table watching television while we eat out breakfast. Then we spend another hour or two travelling in our car or the train on the way to work; to only sit in a chair for another few hours. We repeat this at morning tea, then lunch, only for us to sit down yet again on the commute back home. After returning, we lay down to watch tv and eat dinner, then stay there for the rest of the right. This sitting is the sole reason for half our muscle pain.

Opening up the hips, not only strengthens your glutes and hamstrings, but in my experience, also relieves pain away from your lower back and knees.

The abdominals. They are called the core for a reason. Think of it as the 'structure' to the house that is your body. Without it, everything above or below it is worse off.

Now, I could provide you with various techniques and exercises, but I'd rather you show the interest to research and experiment on your own. Refer to the process of self-learning. Ultimately, it is you who is doing the work. (See disclaimer page 196).

Remember the breathing technique from earlier? This can also be applied to your warm up.

Note: The key is to gradually ease into this. Just add one thing again and again each morning and your will have a routine before you know it. You go all out straight off and you will lose interest and fall back into your old habits of deprivation. Believe me.

Lack of Motivation/Excitement

With all the progress and momentum that you are to build up over the course of your journey, it is only inevitable that eventually, you will become stuck within a new cycle of growth. Your bad habits and way of thinking will start to adapt, and eventually, without you even realizing, your false-self will have worked its way back into your reality. As a result, more often than not, there will be times in your process of transformation where you will feel unmotivated and bored. After the idealized reality that I had consumed my conscious with shattered before me, I lost all interest in doing anything. All motivation, inspiration, and excitement. Gone. With no clear path insight for me to consummate my goal, I had convinced myself that there was no point to go in that direction. Even when I literally sat myself down to pursue anything related to my dream. Nothing. Hours would go by and I wouldn't have crafted anything of any worth. What was I doing wrong?

Getting Comfortable

Tying directly into boredom and aloneness, a lack of motivation means that you have become too comfortable in your situation. Most often we become so consumed by our current lifestyle, we think if I just be patient, things will eventually fix themselves. You can stay in this state simply because you can. There is no force that requires you to move on. It isn't do or die. In this state there is no need for discipline, no lust or passion, and certainly no desire or hunger.

Comfort is good though? Comfort means I am living in the moment, which is a state all must achieve? Yes, it is crucial to live in the moment, but not to the point where you become passive and watch life sail by. Where one day, you wake-up and wonder where it has all gone? Referring back to the rollercoaster metaphor, being comfortable can mean just simply coasting through life passively, with no real influence into what happens to you. You become comfortable with your situation and as a result, the pathway towards opportunity goes stale. The state of flow is blocked. Yes, you can live comfortably out of choice, provided this choice is founded on positive action, then passive reaction. You have to give something in order to receive. There is the point where everything must evolve. Everything must be in a constant state of growth and development.

You may however, be scared, not knowing your next move. That is okay, but don't dwell on it. Remember the section of letting the outcome appear. Often this fear turns to self-doubt, and we question it. In that split second moment of inquisitiveness, the opportunity has passed, and the cycle starts again. So how do you stop this from reoccurring?

Flipping the Script: Using This as Fuel

When you fall back into this state of unhappiness and habit, it may feel like all your progress was for nothing. I am here to tell you, rather than seeing it as a negative, a fire that will quickly eat away at you, use it as fuel to start the engine up again. All it takes is a change in outlook and understanding, to and do what is called *flipping the script*. This term also ties in with bringing everything back to you. Putting first things first. As stated, a lack of motivation and passion for something generally indicates an excess of comfort in your life. The main reason this has formed is the type of environment one situates themselves in. An environment where distractions provide no real relationship between you and the task. No deeper levels and meaning to as why you are undertaking it.

A main component of flipping the script, is to do something that involves a new environment, one that signifies the attributes associated with your true-self. Be it joining a gym to become healthier, conducting research and writing at the local library, or becoming a part of a club that shares your interests with new people.

Sometimes, when we know we don't hold direct responsibility of our environment and actions, we can truly put our full attention to the mission at hand. It is when our mind gets easily put off track, that we tend to focus on what we are not doing and how to do it, rather than just doing. I find I can focus more in one location, minus distractions, than a room that has multiple functions. The number of pages I have completed of this manuscript from writing outdoors and my local library compared to my room is astounding.

Note: I easily could have put this section at the start of this book, however you would have been such at a state, that you would see this as too great a challenge to undertake (due to anxiety or doubt in social situations). You should be at the point in your transformational journey where you don't view this as an obstacle greater than you, but an opportunity that is given to you.

The 15- 30 -15 Method

Have you ever come away from time within a task (be it staring at a computer screen, or book), only to look at the clock to be shocked to find how much time has passed? Fifteen minutes becomes an hour. One hour becomes three. Before you know it, half the day is gone in negative flow, and your motivational levels are non-existent. Why is this?

Your mind is not being stimulated both authentically and actively. It is on cruise control. Auto-pilot. Motivation and inspiration will only propel you so far. To extend beyond the confines of a mental drought, you need to implement a strong routine founded by discipline and consistency. To create a schedule where you set out a time slot every day for your goal. Choose a location where there were no distractions, little people, and where you knew that was all you could do. Right now, I am writing this in my own public library. It is as if the atmosphere is inviting me to write, instead of me wasting creative energy trying to force it elsewhere.

A technique, that you probably have heard before, is to break up your day into hours. I would suggest to take this one step further. Break up the hour.

1. The first five are used for minimal tasks such as chores and lunch breaks.
2. Follow up this with thirty minutes of continuous work.
3. After this, do something for another fifteen to break up the monotony. Get a drink of water or go for a walk.
4. After the hour, flip the script by completing another main task. This time for thirty minutes, then a fifteen-minute break, then finally back to thirty.

The cycle should then reset based on what came before. **15,30,15** then **30, 15, 30**, then **15, 30, 15** and so on.

Note: There will become a point in your duty of coping that you will cross. It is your conscious whispering to you that things have you should immediately stop what you are doing and change your setting. To create some excitement in smaller chores, realise that it is your thought of doing these tasks that ultimately stops you from starting them. Treat it as a miniature session of active mediation. Just start the task, immerse yourself in the most simplistic thing. Before you know it, you will be finished, and before it has even had a chance to form, you wonder what the fuss was about.

Remember Your Goal

Whenever you feel stuck or start to go back into your false habits and ways of thinking, the best response is to offset these thoughts with other ones. Thoughts with the underlying question being asked; What would my true self do? Recall the scenario I asked you to imagine at the beginning of this book? The true self that you know lingers inside? No matter how far away your dream seems, it is still there. Just buried under harsh reality, negative thinking and self-doubt. The biggest mistake that I made upon realizing the harsh reality that underlined my dream, was that I abandoned them. To me the dream no longer existed. It seemed so far away. The important thing to note is that unlike last time, where you were totally lost and consumed by it, you need to reset it in reality. Remember your house and its foundation.

You need to go through these periods of unsureness. It is a reminder that things have grown stagnate and you need to start again. Ironically, or perhaps indefinitely, you are brought back to the place that started you on this journey. Your true-self. If you are still struggling to find inspiration, reflect on the emotions directly at play. All true artists are driven by their honest emotions. Their intent. When you are inspired creatively, it is most of the time caused through the excitement of the image that we paint in our mind. Glamorized in its glory. So vivid and crystal clear, it moves us along effortlessly. As you will read in the chapter on *Sexual Experiences,* the term *inspired* correlates deeply to the purpose of the work. Why are you ultimately doing this?

The Process of Self-Learning
(A Deeper Look Into Practice Makes Perfect)

Throughout my entire structured tertiary experience, I held an underlying feeling that I was not stimulated enough with what I was being taught. Sure, I was learning the content and completing assessments, but there was always this underlying inclination that there was no real relation between myself and the material. That, if I wasn't obligated to be here, I wouldn't actually be interested in learning. Think back to your schooling days (or perhaps you don't need to if you are currently there). Most of the time you were/are not excited by what was/is being taught. From a teacher's perspective it is up to the student to interpret information in a way they understand. To show discipline, the willingness to learn. However, the reason they don't show these qualities is because either they are not at the right point to learn, or the content isn't being taught in a way that warrants stimulation.

Structured learning often revolves around the teacher's viewpoint onto the student (even though they are going off a planned syllabus). The issue that often arises with institutional learning, is that it is based on the mantra that one size fits all. It is not malleable to every type of student and mindset. If they are teaching it, and subsequently the student is learning it because the institution dictates so, it becomes stale, without meaning; thus, obtainable only for a select few. It ultimately becomes a challenge for those who struggle to grasp the content quickly. It was only out of formal study, that I found a sense of freedom and desire to learn. No longer did it feel like an obligation to study, rather an act I undertook to investigate further into a-part of myself. To be, (first and foremost) my own teacher. It is very easy to forget that different people learn in different ways, and are at different points to learn specific detail. The following highlights the various stages of the process that is required in the mastering an artform in relation to understanding yourself. All knowledge is self-knowledge. Meaning how you interpret it. How you understand it in relation to your own context.

MINDSET

If you focus excessively on techniques prior to understanding their relevance, your mind will be become overwhelmed. Having the proper mindset involves clearing the noise and finding the purpose behind what you are doing. Your task at hand. Imagine yourself confident and in total control. Project this reassurance into your existence. Watch someone performing at the highest level. Use this as inspiration for how to conduct the task without thinking.

FOUNDATION OF PRINCIPLES
(Technique)

Technique is important to how you perform, but in order to grasp it, you must understand its relation to your mind and body. When first starting a new skill, (depending on our understanding) we bring over bad habits that are disjointed. Building a strong foundation of principles is a suitable way to establish a relationship built on muscle memory, balance, coordination and connection. The goal here is to achieve the feeling of your body working as a whole unit.

Only work within the bounds that your current skills will allow. Don't run before you can walk. Don't try to paint the Sistine chapel, when you can barely trace the circumference of your own emotions.

INITIAL PRACTICE

Practice the technique to find a connection with the body and ultimately flow into a position of comfort and effortlessness. Go off what feels right rather than what you think is right. Just do what you can and work from there. Each session I try and work through my thoughts and emotions, taking away one detail about my technique that I can relate to this aura of oneness.

PRACTICE WITH ANOTHER

(Resistance to react to)

Now it is one thing to get to a point with your technique alone, it is another thing entirely to have this tested with an outside force. Having another entity with their own mindset and technique forces you to playfully experiment.

Note: Playfully refers to the intention that underlines the level of force. It is reserved. Not under a context where there are any boundaries. If it is an activity that does not involve another (say writing or artwork), this is where another opinion/critique is needed to evolve your skill.

IN GAME ENVIRONMENT

(Resistance without boundaries/control)

All your above steps become irrelevant, as this new environment brings its own variables to adjust to. High-pressured, fast-paced, and some cases, no rules. Therefore, it is guaranteed that there will be elements you were no match/unprepared for. In this instance, you must review your performance and then, repeat the cycle.

Research to fill in the gaps. Articles, videos, new techniques, anything to expand your knowledge and understanding of the task in relation to you. It is the successful combination of mindset and technique, of mind and body, that allows for a complete release of focus. If something feels off, you will have to correct a variable; part of technique/form and reset your bearings to be able to find that state of higher performance again.

If, after everything you are doing still isn't working, break down the activity to its simplest form, and restart from there.

If you are worrying about the little things, to the point it overloads you, take a break from the activity altogether.

Assess the practice. Break it down. Repeat.

Albert Einstein alleged it would take roughly ten thousand hours to master a skill. It is in these ten thousand hours that we are building up the skill completely, and then breaking it down to the point where it is no longer skill, but instinct.

Disclaimer: For Teachers

This may seem like all the responsibility is being held accountable towards the instructor. As a son of parents that were both teachers, I can reassure you this is not the case. I understand that sometimes there are environments where the dynamic between doesn't always allow for easy teaching conditions. Children, teenagers, and even adults, can be obnoxious, loud, crude and disruptive, and when that is brought to the forefront when a teacher is trying to coheres a large group of diverse personalities, this dynamic can almost be impossible. So, either the teacher (using this as an insightful moment) changes his/her way of presenting the content in a more engaging way, or the student changes his/her approach to learning. Wanting to learn no matter how it is presented. What should also be taught is how to deal with the challenges of learning. Not just the content itself. The process, not the goal.

To work the teachings around the student, as opposed to working the student around the teachings. The student and their own understanding of the information is at the heart of a learning process. This is the ultimate goal for the teacher; to guide the pupil to self-realisation. This is their lesson. It is not what is being taught, but rather **how** it is being taught. Just like it is not what you say, it is how you say it. (Refer to *Saying Things with Conviction*).

Is All This Necessary?

A thought that I believe should be considered is whether all this necessary? I don't mean schools and institutions, but rather the deeper look into learning. From my own experience and self-reflection if I had not experienced the structure of formal education, I would have not have learnt what doesn't work for me. That there is another way. Even though we may fail at a particular way, that in itself is a lesson. A lesson learnt through failure. Once again, it is a process. If only I had been aware of this before, I would have been able to make the most of my schooling experience. Or perhaps, that was the most that I was ever able to make of it, and that is in itself the lesson. As you might conclude upon reading *(Pathways: Job, College, Career)*, academic study is not suited to everyone, which is okay. What is suited to and available to everyone however, is the pursuit of understanding your own true self.

They say it are the organizations/systems that need changing. That producing specific options and outcomes is all down to the framework. What we are forgetting is who follows, upholds and dictates the successful/unsuccessful functioning of all these? People. Organizations are made up of people. Change the system they say. What does this mean? Rework the framework to support diversity? Or cull the people that improperly allow newcomers to function in a set operation? Perhaps it is the corrupt leaders that need to change.

Maybe it's you, the individual struggling to enter.

How To Achieve True Focus

Whenever I undertook a task that I knew was for my benefit, but was backed by long moments of isolation, I would most often lose focus very quickly. Those rare accounts where I did finish a session, I still managed to come away never feeling truly satisfied, almost questioning did I even do anything?

Much to contrary of what is stressed in this book, which empathizes branching awareness, when it comes to focus and being completely lost in a task, this is the one instance where it is advised to focus one's thought precisely.

Perhaps one of the most useful concepts when referring to the practical application of higher being, is progressive focus. I can recount various times playing sport, where I took a distinct note of making mistakes compared to when I was playing well. Surely there must be something I was missing?

Often times, we feel we can just ride this good fortune as chance, that it comes and goes. Well, I am here to tell from experience, it is something we can in fact harness to use on command.

We can illustrate this with the concept of progressive focus, through the use of three levels (or tiers), each symbolizing the different states of when you aren't in focus, to when you are. An appropriate analogy that most can relate to, is the spatial awareness one unknowingly moves through whilst playing a sport.

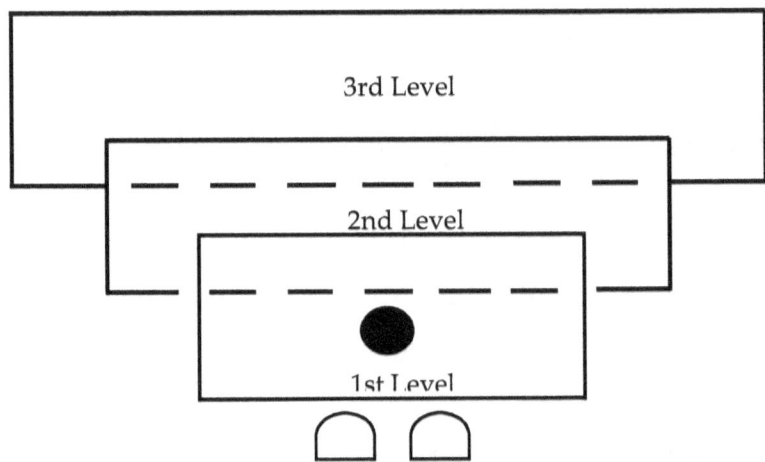

1st Level: You constantly must look down at the ball to execute the task. This is a reflection that you are too concerned with the technique behind the action. Your focus is thus too short and needs to expand its horizon.

2nd Level: This is what we can classify as headspace or subconscious focus. Your gaze is looking up, but not open. It is kind of in a mid-limbo, a no-man's-land, where your mind is too concerned with the outcome and the other player's actions. The second tier especially makes you come across as awkward and creepy and reflects on your mental state. Naturally your instinct is to go from this tier to the first, by glancing down at the ground. This only makes it worse. People with self-doubts and no confidence will resort two either tiers one or two, acting as if they are embarrassed and uncomfortable to showcase their presence. Note the focal range. You can see, but all your attention is going on in your head. Interestingly, referring back to branching awareness, depending on the context, there will be times where a narrow viewpoint will be needed (as if the model is reversed). Whether it be watching the ball before you kick it, or looking at someone's eyes when speaking, sometimes focus isn't about focusing at all. It is about being with what is front of you.

3rd Level: True Focus. You are completely honed in on the moment. Your task at hand. You are confident. Not cocky. Calm. Think of it like driving a car. You have to make clear decisions and not hesitate in the slightest. You have no time to. Now that you are in this state, your whole depth of field is tripled (unless you are nearsighted), with your entire body acting as one unit. You aren't concerned with technique or the outcome; you are just in the moment. You and the task are in harmony. Not fighting to gain control. By looking up and ahead, you will also naturally correct your posture and walking style. By glancing forward instead of down, (focusing on tucking the chin), you aren't concerned with what others think or affected by their actions. In the chakra system, there is a channel known as the 'third eye' (you may be more familiar with the central red dot). Located on the forehead, this symbolises the higher perception and awareness one can look through. No longer are you perceiving things through your eyes, which are susceptible to illusion, but a much broader course of vision. "Well, that's great", you may say. "But how do I get to that tier from where I am?"

Emotional Content (What it Means to Express Yourself)

This is a term I find applies to not just training, but life in general. Work, relationships, anything and everything you undertake. It is the invisible force behind why we are in such a state of pure effortlessness and flow. Thinking without thought, whilst having thought without thinking. Emotional content ties directly with the feeling that is to be 'in the moment'.

Sub-conscious, consciousness or conscious, sub-consciousness.

or

1. Not worrying or having fear about what could happen.
2. Not trying to impress anyone or fuel your ego.
3. Asking yourself, what is my task at hand?

or

Your relationship to it.

Rather than your inner conscious driving the action, be it worry, fear or the ego, emotional content refers to the subconscious decisions that is outwardly displayed almost immediately, without hesitation. This connection ties directly to the principle of genuine intention i.e., why you are doing it, however, with this comes an extremely fine line to balance across. We confuse emotional content, with emotional behaviour. The major one being anger. Yes, anger is an emotion, but it is also an action, a verb. A direct consequence to what is happening inside, displayed openly. Sometimes, it is purely animalistic instinct that takes over and we become a being without thought or control. (See *When to Stand Up for Yourself*). It sounds very condescending, I know. Have emotional content, but don't use emotion that is driven by what's inside. It is very much dependent on the situation where too much can mean excess, and too little can mean substandard performance. All requires the right mix of reading the situation and having the right awareness to your potential reaction. (See *How to the Read Situation & Act Accordingly*).

Update: When I first heard the term emotional content, I subconsciously attached to it with what I thought was a correct definition. I was saying it, but not really However, once I had finished this book, and given time to process and develop, I found the explanation given did not do it justice, and thus a slight change was needed. Emotional content is, above all, <u>the outward expression of your essence</u>. The flair of YOU, the individual. The individual who gets scared, who shows caution, who strives for more, who sees the humour in things. The individual, who realizes, after reading this book, that their success was ultimately not achieved by any path, or way that was followed, but the soul that was able to do so. That to 'me', is the 'true' definition of emotional content. What is it for you?

The Antidote to Fear

The Christmas eve of me finishing the first draft of this book, a litter of mice sprung from a chest of draws in my parent's bedroom. Scattering throughout the various rooms of our house, we sought to drive them out over the next couple of days, culminating to where we weren't sure how many remained. One night, there I was laying on my bed when out of the corner of my eye, a quick flash of fur ran across the wooden floorboards. Immediately I resorted to my usual response. Fear. Honestly, I am surprised I hadn't included this topic earlier on. Perhaps, because given the diversity of content, fear resides at the root of them. Rejection. Failure. Loss. Being wrong. Hurting someone. Snakes. Spiders. Skydiving Oh my! After, dissecting the extent of my own observations on it across multiple scenarios and contexts, I found despite it being something reserved for these tangible objects, most often than not, it isn't the object itself that we fear, but the uncontrollable aspects associated with it. The underlying notion of the unknown. For example, I have always had a fear of heights, well, not the fear of skyscrapers and being above looking down, but rather the fear of falling. The aftermath. The potential for injury. The repercussions of my demise. It is that unknown element to the object/situation that drives the experience of hysteria and vertigo.

Circle of Anxiety: Visualize a circle out in front of you. Anything outside this space, be it a person, an object or a situation, you need not fear. The key is to not see it as such. See the thing that you are afraid of in a different light.

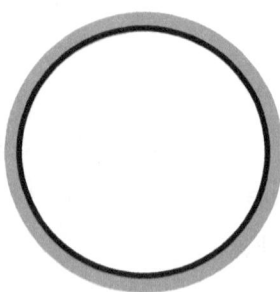

So, as I now had nowhere to go, I was forced to sit atop my bed and watch the floor for any sign of movement. On the edge of the wall opposite my bed, was a bookshelf with some cushions stacked atop. Soon enough, in all its innocence, the mouse emerged from the shadows. I laid still, doing nothing but watch it stare directly at me from across the room. Its beady eyes glimmering into my own, it was as if all the fear that I had accumulated over the years was for in vain. I saw it as an entity with its own life. Its own experience. My perception of that mouse had changed. **Note:** There is a difference between being cautious, and fearful. I have never been petrified of snakes or spiders to the point where I cower in terror, but I do understand that they (depending on the species) are dangerous, sickly and unpredictable. Therefore, the fear is not fear based on cowardness, but a lack of control, and understanding.

Circle of Control: Now visualize an inner circle. Tight to your body. Almost too close to see. It is there though. This space represents that everything inside here is what you have control over.

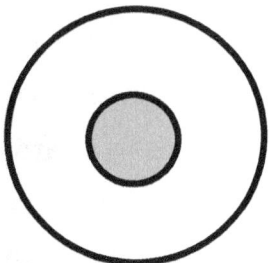

Think, play it close to you, under your eyeline, the body working tight as one unit. Everything that happens to you results from how you accept, reject or relay things between these circles. Say you are afraid of a person. When they aren't looking, stare at them for a couple of seconds. Let all your doubt settle along with any outside thoughts or opinions. See them in the light the sun shines on them, not the one you cast over. Soon the fear that consumed you, will turn to freedom. The next time you find yourself overly nervous when going into a situation, confronting a person or concerned about the outcome of a particular moment, exclaim to yourself; "Yes, I am afraid. Yes, I am anxious of the unknown". Accept and acknowledge your emotions. Every time you try to wrap your brain around searching for an escape, you only trap yourself even further from passing through between experiences, into the moment. The sooner you let go of the 'what if', the sooner you can concentrate on doing what is needed, and nothing else.

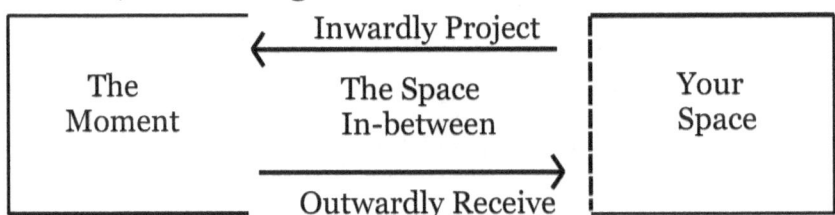

Ultimately you will discover this state of being will no longer necessarily be something you get to. It will evolve to something you now are. You do get there technically from being in another state, but as a result of implementing all other teachings you have learnt thus far. No distractions or foul habits. Just having genuine intention and branching out your awareness. This is the natural effect and result. Having a calm mind free of thought, but full of emotional content is key. Keep relaxed, not tense, but ready. When your muscles are all locked up by your thoughts of 'what if', the task at which you so desire to achieve has no chance of using its key to come in. A great que to simply ask yourself; what is my task at hand? Again, in note of the sports metaphor; you have the ball and need to score to win. So, do.

Standing Up For Yourself
(Controlling Your Rage, Anger and Frustration)

Being the smallest kid on the playground, it wasn't uncommon, on occasion, for my peers to take advantage of me. "He wouldn't fight back. He's too nice". The truth was I did want to fight back. Badly. However, even with a 'hands' off policy at the school, I knew (being the forward thinker) any attempt to stand up for myself and show any retaliation would be pointless. I would push back, resulting in me being sent to the principal's office, which would only then involve my parents. It seemed more logical to just let them do it, and go on with the day.

Not this particular day though (a week prior to writing this). The morning of any seemingly normal football match. Overcast. A slightly muddied field. An unofficial referee (supervising member on the opposing team), reminding us to play fair, and be honest. What could go wrong? The match started out as per usual with a lack of enthusiasm, communication and cohesion from my team mates. Not until the opposing team scored off a blatant off-side ruling that was 'overlooked' by the 'referee', did things go south.

A moment emerged late in the second-half, where I was in a desperate chase against another player. Calm and collected, he shielded himself and the ball with his body. Almost in a taunting way as if I was a child, he started to laugh at me. Frustrated at the fact of being forced off the ball, in a team disjointed in their harmony, and losing all because of the dishonesty of a cheating referee, I was already on a knife's edge. Then, it happened. He stood on my hand.

"Okay, that's fine", I thought as I started to regather myself. Wham! Suddenly his fist forced my head directly into the dirt. Any other time, I would have just done nothing. Let the situation pass, and leave them thinking all their pre-conceptions about me were right. However, from the instant I started to get up, to the second it took to walk over, I knew that moment had passed. Suddenly, like another person had taken control of my body, I leapt up in surge of rage. Emotions running high, I immediately followed the player back to his side of the field.

"Don't touch me"! I commanded sternly. His body, still facing me, stopped.

"What are you going to do?" He was a-few good inches taller than me. Not especially stocky or anything, just someone, who if equally was in a fit of rage, could easily overpower me. I took a step towards him, about a metre's length separating us. With ferocity in my eyes, I pointed my finger in his direction.

"I'll rip your F@#$%&* throat out." Now, I was never actually going to rip someone's throat out. Although I had studied martial arts for years, (as I found a sense of confidence and understanding of my body I never had before), this was more a tactic to put him in his place. Plus, it wasn't just me and him. There was a whole team surrounding me at his side ready. It was during this time that my conscious had switched from aggression with action to retractable reaction. I had made my point. My eyes however, were still scanning the movements of his body.

Out of my peripherals, I could see his right foot take a step forward towards me. I switched my stance from a forward left leg to right, angling myself at the ready position. It was at that moment I saw his right hand move from his side upwards towards my body. In that fraction of a split second, I threw forward a straight lead with my right hand in his general direction. It was a pulled punch, meaning I did not follow through with the blow, as I was still consciously aware of the consequences and context of the situation. Though, in that small flash of time I had seen his hand and threw my own, I had escalated the situation further than it needed to go. Immediately, an opposing player launched himself at me from the left. Again, he was a few inches taller than me, although this time, it worked in my advantage. I went with it, feeling his force to roll out, distancing myself from the large group of people.

The reality of the situation came forward to my mind. I realised what I was doing. Another player, (again from the opposing team), came running from the bench. Smaller in stature, but stockier, he came to rest his hand on my shoulder. "It's alright, he said. It's okay". I took that moment to distance myself from my emotions. He was right.

Having calmed down, I retreated to the side-line. Continuing to play would only have exacerbated the situation. Ironically, another one of our players who was prone to starting confrontations, was now in one with another member of the opposition. Immediately I felt a wave of embarrassment wash over me, almost ashamed for doing it. Not allowed or worthy to just because of my smaller frame. It all happened so fast though! Over the next couple of days, I thought deeper about it, pondering the prior cause and latter effects. I came to a startling conclusion. Me being perceived as someone who was not able to stand up for themselves in such a manner was a good thing. It gave me a better weapon at my disposal.

Letting It Go/Picking Your 'Fights'

We become so offended by a remark that questions our actions and integrity, that we never truly ask ourselves if the situation warrants or justifies the response. By reacting to it in anger, we only provide the answer. Ask yourself. Given the weight of your outburst, is there any hint of truth to the comment? At all? If there is no truth to it, you know they are saying it to mask the falseness of themselves. There is nothing to be offended of, as nothing officially offensive was said.

Anger can be useful to put someone in their place. To shock or teach an insightful lesson. However, we misinterpret this, (like I was, consumed by rage), to lash out physically. The player who came over to calm me understood. He knew the **context in which my rage was brought upon**. This is my advice to you. Be offensive, by being indifferent. The more you become aware of this, the more you will be able to react accordingly without conflict. The next time the seeds of anger became apparent through my own frustrations, I realised this and took a moment to settle. Don't let people walk over you, but if they do, know the right time and effort to trip them from under their own feet.

As said by the character Socrates, in Dan Millman's novel, *Way of the Peaceful Warrior*; **"The wisdom of life is learning to apply the right leverage in the right place at the right time"**. Sometimes that right time is just to put out your hand, talk calmly, then walk away.

Having Sex vs. A Sexual Experience

Apart from love, sex is the other aspect of our lives that we seem to put on a pedestal of such high regard. It makes men fall weak at the knees. Gives women a power, that for years laid dormant. The act of pleasure that in most cases drives every underlying decision we make when it comes to satisfaction. The act so good, we can't live without.

Why then, do so many of us have a lack lustre experience?

I can tell you from the observations of my own sexual encounters (if you can even call them that), the overall experience was nothing short of underwhelming. Sure, things were happening, but I felt nothing, and I mean nothing. At all. Even worse, it because of this lack of sensation that I was always left wondering. Where was this excitement and pleasure I was promised?

During my second time round of online dating (coming from a five-month abstinence from my addictive state), I found myself talking to a girl whom I had not had the pleasure of meeting yet. My mind was completely free of pre-judgement and expectation, my only thought of her given by an initial photo. One night out of the blue, she called me, something girls never did. Ever. I was always making the first move, always putting in the effort but never getting that reciprocation back (I now understand why). Nether the less, this startling event led to us talking further, and as the night progressed, and we started flirting, things changed direction.

Suddenly I felt the odd sensation of my stomach tightening and my head feeling light. My legs began to shake and my breath became shorter and heavier. My body was struggling to remain upright on the lounge chair I was sitting on, and I wasn't even doing anything. Just listening. Now ironically, much to my dismay, when I did meet her in person, she was not of the same energy as I had experienced that night. I just didn't feel the dynamic. I had created an expectation in my mind of what she should have been based on what I deemed attractive. Based on a photo. The question still remained. What was that other worldly experience that came through me that night?

Over the next couple years, I sought to reset my thought patterns and abolish all disillusioned associations with sex I had unknowingly accumulated. I went back to my grandmother's table, coming across a particular cover that, any other time, I would not have any interest in picking up. With my newfound direction of becoming extensively aware, I was open to everything and anything that would aid my cause. The work in particular, titled *Going Within: A Guide to Inner Transformation,* was by acclaimed author and actress, Shirley MacLaine. In it, she writes directly about the connection between the spiritual in ones-self and sex.

"We use sexual attraction to choose people with whom we can resolve these issues; lacks, the unfulfilled needs, and the angers in our psyches. We can be sexually attracted to someone because we sense in the person a problem that is a reflection of our own trouble, and sex becomes the excuse and the bridge to intimacy. No longer is it so direly necessary to seek and find a partner to fulfill one's physical needs. Self is becoming fulfilled and more clarified within. People are feeling more consummated in

themselves; therefore, when they find themselves attracted to another, the relationship becomes a bonding out of equal recognition rather than bonding through fear and a sense of need and loneliness,".

This statement here I feel is the difference between **simply having sex, and a sexual experience**. A difference we, for the most part, are not aware exists. It certainly wasn't for me. We put sex on this giant pedestal that it is the single most glorious thing, without realizing the context and variables that it takes to manifest.

Are You Truly Aroused?

How many times have you heard a man say, "I faked an orgasm"? "What? No! That's impossible! That's only something women do. They are the only ones capable". To the contrary, I believe in most cases, men almost ninety percent of the time fake an orgasm, yet in their moment of submission, are unaware that they do so. Too conditioned through subconscious, conscious thought. Although they are in the act of sexual intercourse, they are still consciously awake, comparing to either what they have seen online and/or too caught up in their quest for dominance and performing correctly. They think just because they are 'doing it', it automatically makes it viable, and thus a pleasurable, satisfying experience. This also applies to women, yet as you will later read, the context surrounding it will be slightly different.

In most instances, I could easily replace 'they' with 'I', as looking back, these were a part of my own experience. Every-time, there was always this shadow of doubt that forced me to question. Was I truly aroused? Or was I aroused, on the **basis that it was meeting my expectation?**

Sex should not feel like a duty, a means to easily expel energy and feel good **about yourself**. It is an opportunity to join into the space where one can express their mind and body **with another**. The problem with that however is with that opportunity, comes a means of misinterpreting, and misusing it. For example;

1. Someone who is physically aroused, but is emotionally not invested. (Gratifying the desires of the ego).
2. Two people who are physically aroused, but not emotionally invested.
3. One person who is only physically aroused, while the other is emotionally invested. (Taking advantage of their naiveite).

This last dynamic is the one that promotes the most confusion. There are those that, sure, are able to have a glorious physical response, however is this at the expense of the other's own pleasure?

The <u>feeling</u> of being aroused, is different to being truly aroused.

Relationship expert, life coach and sexual educator, Ken Blackman openly discusses the interplay between pleasure and desire. He illustrates a highly revealing exercise that I found answered my lacklustre experiences surrounding the physical component of arousal.

"Hold your arm out, palm up, and use your other hand to trace slow, very light circles around the inside of your elbow. Use the lightest touch you can, barely brushing the hairs on your skin. Notice the tingling, almost ticklish feeling? Almost as if your skin is reaching

for more? Do this for a while, and notice how the sensation changes. When you're done, you can go ahead and rub or massage it out. And as you do, notice what that feels like. Very different, maybe like scratching an itch, more grounding. An exhale to the bated breath of the first one. The idea is that there can be touch that creates a desire for more touch... and touch that satiates. The first can be enjoyably tantalizing for a bit, but if you do it for too long eventually it can become irritating or aggravating".

As a result of becoming extremely desensitized to what you may view a substitute for real intimacy and reciprocation, you go through a gradual change where your perceptions of what sex actually involves is both narrow and limited. It is completely different once you are there in person, and having to rely on all your senses. From the depth perception of you looking at your partner, the aroma of the air, the subtle taste of their lips, the feeling of their body, and the sound of your pleasure. All the little things don't impress you anymore, and thus, you need to delve into rougher ideologies to 'satisfy' your needs (even then you could argue that it's simply because you associate it with being pleasurable). From experience, this approach caused my sensitivity levels to become greatly affected, to the extent where instead of the slightest touch (like Blackman suggests) causing arousal, it's like rubbing against sandpaper. Eventually the feeling numbs out. As a male whose receptors have now been reset to normal, a small glimpse of a woman is enough to stimulate the senses. You see something attractive that provides the initial moment needed to spark a response. It may be as subtle as skin, a laugh, smile, hair, a voice (this was the leading contribution to my experience over the phone). However, from a woman's perspective, this is the norm. It requires a lot more for the female to be turned on. They need substance. They need emotional content. If only we were to understand that sex is never about you, or them. It isn't even about the sex. It just is. The 'space' between that magically draws you to the ecstasy that is being with another. The two forced pushing and pulling. It will naturally be about you and them all at the same time! I believe his space is the key in allowing a true experience to unravel, as opposed to being blocked by our pre-conditioned conscious.

Take the act of kissing. You never kiss with your eyes open. You are one with the moment, savouring the sensational feeling of each other's magnetic pull. Only do you to break and bask in your partner's own acknowledgment of their ecstasy. A sexual experience should be just that. You should not be consciously awake with your eyes open, (or your mind), but subconsciously free. Experiencing the feeling of the touch, intimacy, of two bodies uniting.

There was such a disconnect between my mind and body, that I never could have reached the experience that I so desired; a total out of body experience. Not because it simply, 'feels good'. I realised then and there in order to have a fully three-dimensional experience, I had to expel from my mind the idea of sex itself, and the pleasures associated with, and **first** focus on the dynamic that should exists between each person, before, during and after.

The Dynamic: Masculinity & Femininity

The dynamic, to me, was crucial in helping me understand how truly genuine sex occurs, and at the same time, why it doesn't. Referring back to the types of dynamics that love can form, it could very well be illustrated through another equation; however, I feel in this particular case, the outcome of the sum of both variables (satisfying sex) is one that is a very slippery slope. In order to differentiate, it is crucial to understand the biological roles of male and females, and the proper power dynamic that should exist between the two. Stay with me now. Remember, don't let your pre-positioned judgements and attachment to terms cloud your judgement. It's important not to see this through rose-coloured eyes of stereotype, rather the meaning behind it that drives both masculine and feminine. It is through the understanding of this dynamic that you will be able to have truly honest experiences, based on mutual understanding and equal emotion. Men are naturally more physical, dominant and able to take control of a situation. However, where this becomes a problem, is when it is in excess. Abusive. Rough. Lacking compassion. You may have heard the term 'toxic masculinity' before. I can see where this originated from, and while I believe there is merit to this, I feel the more appropriate term to use would be **excess masculinity**. You may have heard the phrase 'get in touch with your feminine side'. Although there is much disagreement by what defines this, it ultimately means understanding the needs of women and knowing how to properly treat them. Respecting them not as a female, but as a human first. Men can be romantic, compassionate, creative, affectionate and understanding, and that doesn't mean for an instant it is feminine, and therefore weak. It is masculine in its femininity. What is however, is being needy, indecisive, and overly emotional. Call this **unrefined masculinity**. For some, the mention of such word becomes a turn-off. Do not see it as being masculine, rather just you as a person working on your lagging traits to become whole. Refining the masculine in oneself, to the point where it evens out the feminine so that you aren't being consumed by your emotions and vice versa. **Therefore, feminine is masculine, and masculine is feminine.** They are one of the same. What separates them is the **context, and amount in which they exist**.

With the movement of social rights and equality now providing much needed avenues and options for women, I feel some have misinterpreted this as being the same as men, and a result, have taken the opportunity to instil the same one-dimensional thoughts that have been conditioned into men. In order to be accepted, they believe they have to portray themselves as overtly sexual, and in doing so, lose apart of themselves just for the approval of men, and society in general. They see being a powerful woman as taking advantage of a weakness that subside in men when it comes to sex. "Taking control of my sexual life to get what I want". Now while, it is perfectly fine for women to feel confident and comfortable sexually (in their bodies), with this sudden intake of egotistic energy, the scales have become unbalanced. It only cheapens their power. Truly respectful authority come from the ability to **appropriately** choose when and to whom you give that part of yourself to. Replace sexuality with sensuality. It is subtle. Generates mystery. The body is secondary to the overall presentation of yourself. A deputy role, to the sheriff that is your soul.

There are double standards you may say, and indeed they are, but looking at things from a worldly view, these standards apply both to male and female, spread by context. Remember;

You are a human being first.
A male or female (gender second)
A title (cultural identity) third.

A strong woman is one who has the ability to have the pleasure of any man, but chooses not to act on it, just simply because she can. Just solely to please her ego. She selects a partner for not what he can give her, but for whether his morals and standards line up with her own. Now, the man does hold an equal responsibility in this.

Being a strong male is exactly the same as what it means to be a strong female. It means having the choice to select a partner that possesses qualities that mirror his own. A lesser male will choose based on surface level qualities, wanting to gain something from the other. i.e., sex. He is going off his primal urges, which although natural, only reflects his neediness. He has willingly let this happen to him, but rather than question why it was so easy, in the gratification of his desire he fails to become aware of one thing. That the experience he is involved in isn't based on recognition and respect. It isn't equal. Rather a fallacy that is based upon an illusion. We all have these natural urges that are biologically programmed into us, but ironically, in delving into them, we have forgotten the proper form they should exist under.

Instead, we have created a dynamic that really isn't a dynamic at all, but a cycle that continues to swirl.

The sexual weakness of man is created by strong/weak women who in turn, are created by strong/weak men through <u>consensually accepting</u> them.

And

The sexual weakness of women is created by strong/weak men who, in turn, create weak women through <u>knowingly preying</u> on them.

This cycle is prevalent upon what society defines 'strong' as, and what the individual interprets 'strong' as. Weak can mean two things. Innocent to their limits, and ignorant to the truth.

How To Break It?

If men were only able to grab control of their urges and desires, then this in turn would force women to elevate themselves to a higher standard, not just flaunting their assets. Then, by females having more control and being less excessive in their sexuality, it will in turn result in males having to elevate themselves to a higher standard. Both 'choose' but it's not done in a way where it is based on wanting. They decide based on the mutual understanding that exists between the two. When either of these powers are exploited, abused or used under false egotistic intentions, the relationship is ruined. This here reflects a major form of disinformation that is out there when it comes to the intentions of people when it comes to sex. Intentions, that, if viewed from the wrong perspective, can mean all the difference between satisfaction while doing, and consequences after completion.

"The more we each resonate to the perfection of the Higher Self, the more we are reflecting perfect balance in ourselves, the more androgynous we are. This does not mean bisexual. It simply means perfectly balanced recognition of the feminine and masculine aspects in each of us". – Shirley MacLaine

It Has to Be Earnt

Whenever I would interact with a new person where potentially things could happen, ironically, the dynamic never quite added up to the extent where I could just relax and let go. Either, they were people whom I found sexually attractive, yet were turned off by their personality, or they were sweet people (a personality I was greatly drawn to), but not matter how I tried to convince myself, I did not find them sexually attractive. It felt as if I instigated everything, always taking the lead, I would be taking advantage of them. Naturally, my mind would jump forward to the events of 'what if', desperately trying to work my way back to the variable that would make it happen. Alas, that final piece that I so desired always alluded me. What was that bridge that connected the two together?

In his book, *The Way of the Superior Man*, David Deida provides an insightful statement that was this bridge. One word actually. *Inspired*. Not because you are feeling down, doing it to cope, or out of loneliness, but because your body feels inspired to. He repeats this phrase over again and again, relating it the habits of masturbation and arousal levels.

In Taoist philosophy, there is the belief that a man's semen is his life force, his chi energy. Expelling this energy on false grounds of arousal, attraction and genuine connection, is a waste of his liveliness. It was no coincidence, that whenever I did such, I felt no better than before I started. From a physiological standpoint, masturbation for example, can ease physical stresses, such as migraines, but now with it such a common occurrence, this line can become blurred. Stress itself can be purely based on elements of frustration, neediness and being overwhelmed. A way to please your receptors to raise the ego (think software vs. hardware). Abolish these initial sensations of the false, and just focus on imagining the genuine dynamic/scenario that should exist as a result of your true self. Treat it like a reset button. Ridding yourself of the internal fallacies, to be ready for a genuine experience.

From a male perspective (although it can apply to women); you may see someone who is physically attractive and immediately jump ahead thinking about what this person can be for you sexually. Whenever these thoughts came into my head, I would remind myself to show a little patience. To let the situation naturally present itself. To give the other person the benefit of the doubt, and see if they would make the move. The more I did this, soon I realised that my desire and arousal were entirely based on my own action. I was aroused, but only because it is serving my own gratification. If I wanted something completely out of my direct control, I had to let it reveal itself to me. I had to earn it.

You Don't Have to 'Love' One another to Have Sex

"What!" You cry out in outrage! "How can you say that?' I hate to tell you, as much as we like to deny it, when it comes to feelings of longing, we see 'love' only under the parameters of marriage, (which of course is justified). However, I feel when viewed only this way, it can force people (who aren't ready for such commitment) into poor sexual situations out of rebellion, forgetting the recognition, respect and mutual understanding that comes with loving. With casual sex, pornography and online dating becoming more widespread, there are people who reply to the above statement by saying; "Yeah, we know". What is more important than the act itself, is what is driving those feelings for the act to occur? What are the factors beyond the surface level? Many identify sex as something that can be categorised into numerous types. Be it tantric, rough, 'first time' or 'make-up', we classify them as being separate. The main distinction on the spectrum being 'making love' and rough animalistic. These false distinctions are more based upon the context of the situation, completely disregarding the factor that should bind them together. Connection.

Comparisons can be made, to the various 'styles' of martial arts. Yes, there are different ways that fighting can be structured under, however taking the context away, there just is fighting. Sex is just the same. It can be passionate, slow, rough, fun and sensual. You can go at different intensities, but what is important that they co-exist together as a part of a longer sequence. Most often we just jump straight in, and start in the middle, missing all the small connective pieces, that in normal circumstances, set up what is to follow. Referring back to the 'space'. It is this that is founded upon by spontaneous action and reaction of two expressing genuine feelings. It both ignites and bridges each part together. Have patience. Lose your desire. Let that space of true sexual tension (intimacy) in. Allow that reciprocation to occur. Refer back to the dynamic though. Is it genuine? There is the notion that we need lust to develop a satisfying experience? I believe the better term, and the aspect of sex we have forgotten, is passion. Passion for the other person, not their assets.

Passion founded on lust is a lie, whilst lust founded upon love, is true passion.

One-Night Stand

Take a one-night stand, that are in most cases, based upon two people being sexually attracted to another. Usually (but not always), this interaction is aided by the influence of alcohol, which depending on their level of toxicity, greatly affects decision making and awareness. Yes, you could say the dynamic is equal and works, but only in its disillusion. Both parties are one dimensionally in it for the surface level. What makes it even worse is the instances where one party wants more (a relationship), and the other backs out. This is where feelings are hurt, emotions run high, and misunderstanding ensues.

Generally speaking, women seek to have a connection before having sex, while men 'need' to have sex to then develop a connection. At first, it would seem that, in order to achieve an honest dynamic, each gender should trade ideologies, with men showing patience to get to know the other person. However, with equality being misinterpreted as a means of taking on both overly refined tendencies, perhaps the better response to have a combination of both. To balance out the scales as opposed to offsetting them.

Although we strive to become equal through dispersing our differences, it is through our differences we realise, in more ways than not, we are already equal. As incomplete people.

Sex has always been a topic that was defined as taboo and awkward to discuss. Yet ironically (and rather sadly), in becoming more open and looser, it has lost its meaning in the sea of fantasy elements, distancing itself from the reality component that is overlooked and integral. At the root of all misinterpretation and misuse of sex (beneath the foundations of loneliness, fear, rebellion and guilt) are these two things. **Intimacy and Reciprocation.** Not desire! Through using this word, we try to cultivate it through any means, and accept it in any form. Drop the desire. Replace it with **appreciation and/or connection**. Refer back to attraction being like a mirror. I now realise the reason why I was having these experiences with the opposite sex I did not find attractive. I was not truly attractive in myself. Therefore, what else was I going to receive? Whenever I was in a state of my true self, I would become noticeable to those whom I did find attractive. Going back to the terms of alpha and beta, we must learn the aspect that we lack within ourselves, and refine it in a way that creates a persona that joins these two forces into one. In regards to sex, when you know that you are starting to give in to your false submissive self (pleasurable of having the feeling gratified), shift the power my tapping into your masculine assertiveness. On the opposing side, when you feel you are too wrapped up in your dominance (same gratification), slow down. Bring it back to the feeling/connection between you and your partner. Let that space grow. Just like the initial interaction and the events leading up to the act itself, truly satisfying sex is a long sequence, with a series of micro moves back and forth between you and the other. The power dynamic is in a constant shift of dominance and submission. It's like a tennis match. Where each takes a turn, but never give up their place fully. As Shirley MacLaine beautifully illustrates;

"*When sex is free of all limitations: power, sadomasochism, humiliation, or possessiveness, it becomes a spiritual act, pure emotion, and hence induces the feeling that the partners are touching God. They feel as though sex is giving them up, not the other way round".*

The crown is the top tier of the chakra system. Apart from enlightenment, they say it also resembles the weightless light headedness, of an authentic orgasm. Going back to whether you need to love someone to have sex with them, I say absolutely you need to love them, but in the moment. Every time.

What If I Am A 'Virgin'?
In today's current societal landscape, the term 'virgin' comes with much stigma and criticism, partly due to the overt notion that it is traditionally reserved as a credence under religion. A belief used to put pressure on those who haven't yet done the deed, it shames and guilts on those who have it out of wedlock. Like discussed earlier, even though my sexual encounters came much later in life (later in comparison to others around me), I was not experiencing the proper levels of pleasure that were promised to me. Partially this was due to the fact that the dynamic always felt off. How could I physically be with someone, when I couldn't even find them attractive? Now you could say this was partially due to false expectations and judgement I put on others, but to me it didn't feel comfortable. Not only did I want to be attracted to the person, but I wanted to reveal to them that this would be my first time, without it causing an issue to them. The years went by where I was constantly subjected to the pressures by society, ultimately questioning whether I was doing the right thing?

The term 'virgin' is just that. A term. Take that away and it is nothing. "If it's nothing, then it doesn't matter how I lose it"?

For some it is very easy to see sex as no big deal, and thus they jump in right away without a thought of consequence. Sex is sex? Better get it out of the way. Our first sexual experience often forms the basis for our entire view of sex to come. It can either excite people to the extent where they don't hesitate, or frighten them away where they despise it. With the introduction of online culture, sex is being used as another form of ego-centred self-gratification. In order to be accepted and deemed worthy by society, you must be attractive to people. If you look deeper, through the layers and facades, it is all because to deal with a part of themselves, be it fear, guilt and the past.

While I would say it doesn't matter how long it takes, I feel what is more important, is the context in which sex occurs. When it comes to the term 'virgin', the key is to take what principles are behind it. Being pure. Pure in yourself, the other and the reasoning behind your connection (genuine intention). For many of you out there who are still 'virgins', who say I'm just waiting for the right person. Good. Just don't simply say that to appease yourself, or use it as an excuse for not putting in the work of self to attract what you are capable of. Not doing it just because you can. Not based on shame, guilt, fear or lack of patience. You ask a lot of people how they lost their virginity, and they reply; "I was drunk". Alcohol is both a natural depressant and a stimulant, this is counterintuitive, as yes you are relaxed, but not thinking, but not in the right ways. This is why, I believe, so many people often regret 'their first time'. Refer back to the two phrases on 'first'. Sex isn't something you lose, like your phone, wallet, or car keys. It's something you give away. What we cannot realise is 'that something' is you. Every time.

How Do I Get Comfortable?

The only way you will be absolutely comfortable, is if you are with someone you can be purely vulnerable with. Someone you can trust. Yes, you do have to be attracted to them, and vice versa, but in order to attract a sexual experience where you will be truly satisfied and at ease, you must be truly satisfied and at ease within yourself. In these cases, **while impotence is the reason for your cautiousness towards sex, it is your cautiousness and worries towards sex that causes your impotence**. No thoughts should be going through your mind. You should not be worried about your body. Both people are on the same page both for themselves **and** the other. All concerns about what happens after should be non-existent. Think of the responsibility that you hold, and the power dynamic that comes with it. Lose yourself in the moment. Everything will sort itself out. Again, if your virginity was something that you do not lose, that would imply that you had lost it at some stage. What about your innocence? You never lose that. It is always there and comes out in many forms. This doesn't mean you surrender yourself to someone submissively. Rather you surrender to the process. Stop getting attached to the idea of sex and virginity. Remember, they are just words. More important is what are behind the letters. Take sex off that pedestal. Put up a new one. Creating your best self. You will find that in time; you will be in a position where it will feel right. You will go higher than you thought that original pedestal could ever go.

ACT IV

Networking Vs. Social Networking

The ability to talk to whoever, wherever and whenever is one that calls out to the longing desires for closeness of any individual. The world, as vast and expansive as it is, is now a close and connected as ever, with the prospect and opportunities that one is able to generate is staggering.

Yet, why is it, despite this cohesion, there is an ever-growing presence of disharmony and unrest between those of a different opinion? With every new piece of technology, there arises the additional set of environmental context and social discourse in which we can surround ourselves with and abide by. It is these new avenues, that while open up convenient ways of doing things, also allow for concealed pathways for anxiety, discrimination, depression and addiction to flourish.

I was introduced to social media when it was just on the precipice of gaining traction. It was, as most things, done purely out of sheer peer pressure and a need to belong. Even though I knew this, I would still ask myself; was this out of obligation, or necessity? Sure enough, a few years later, the machine that was online communication broke off from the orbit of reality, and rocketed upward into its own stratosphere. All the while, here I was left behind on earth.

Why is Messaging Such a Problem?

Social networking/messaging, when viewed in the wrong context, and used with the wrong intentions, can cause great repercussions for an individual's sense of self, and the ways in which they are perceived by others. From my experience, it acts as a safety barrier, one without any direct judgement or face to face consequence.

To give a bit of personal context, this was at the period in time when I was terrified by the prospect of approaching and interacting with people (women in particular). Texting was a way to breach that barrier first hand. However, all this did was make me come across as even more shy and insecure, and in most cases, creepy. Something I could not understand. In my mind, simply because I was able to talk to them, meant things could go the same way if in person. Internally, my intentions were pure, but showcasing this externally was another problem altogether. Especially when I was afraid of rejection. Every time I did meet someone where a genuine conversation was made, I would always receive the following response; "Sure just add me on (insert social media platform here)". From then on, I knew there was no real intention of contacting me, or when I did, no interest in replying.

Now, from one perspective, this was due to my own neediness at the time, and the lack of independency and overall confidence in myself. That being said, the times when I was attempting to act on my independency through creating new contacts and opportunities, it seemed very unfair and almost disheartening. I was sick of the misunderstanding, the constant distraction it was causing. The overbearing pressure it unloaded onto my mind. I had reached breaking point. As long as it was an ever-present existence in my life,

I knew I would be back in this position once again. I was at the crossroads, and for once, I did not hesitate. So, I did what I knew I should have done years ago, but had not out of a skewed sense of compulsion and belonging. I erased it from my life circle. Gone. It was as if a colossal weight had been lifted off my shoulders. Like Sisyphus, the Greek King of Ephyra, I no longer had the doomed monotony of carrying a boulder up the mountain, only for it to fall down time and time again.

How to Text Properly

Much like 'dating', texting should be free flowing and not formed through a series of conscious decisive steps to follow. Rather than giving you an overly complex guide on how to message people, I believe it is far more beneficial to teach you how to reach a place within yourself to be able to approach and communicate to people naturally. The same principle (although different in social context), can be aligned to bullying. Rather than simply having an adult deal with the event straight away (depending on the severity), teach the 'victim' methods to be able to respond appropriately, and then understand why that bullying is taking place. Here is something you can do;

1. Go through all your contacts and only keep those who are in your current existence. By that, I mean only those who are <u>consistently</u> a part of your life circle.

Immediately when I did this, I became much more present in **my** whole situation and to those whom I **could** talk to.

Note: 'Could' is referring to because 'I could'. They were only 'a part of my life', because they were a part of a contact on a screen.

2. Do not text anyone for a week. Only respond to those who **openly text you first**. Furthermore, only respond if you deem the text worthy to reply to. i.e., emergencies and family. Texting should be used to fill in the little inconsistencies of the day. Never to replace a full conversation. Texting can also be addictive, like anything else. Every time you receive a message it gives off a sense of instant gratification, a hit of dopamine to temporarily excite. Yet when you aren't, it ties directly to factors of neediness, feeling of aloneness, and a false sense of contempt.

3. Going back to the golden rule of genuine intention, ask yourself why it is you are texting them? Most times, it will be out of loneliness and guilt, or requirement. In these instances, no longer has it become driven by emotional purpose and intent.

What If They Don't Reply?

"Wait", you exclaim with all your distain for past experiences. "For the amount of time people spend on their phone, it really doesn't take long to reply". While I agree, I would also precipice, by saying; if they don't, then so be it. **People are busy. They have their own life. You should too.** In relation to attraction, people only text when they want something out of that person. Be it because they genuinely like you or a second ulterior motive. It all relates back to yourself. If the other person isn't on the same page, wait for the right opportunity to communicate. It is important not to get hung up about receiving a message, or sending one. This whole concept will be expanded upon in *how to read the situation and act accordingly*, specifically in the idea of replacing tone and reaction, with tempo and rhythm.

On a note for those on the receiving end of people who I was once like. Rather than seeing them an annoyance, someone who isn't even worth the truth, see them as simply being confused, unaware of how their actions are coming across. When you know this, your approach to them will be not one out of disgust or pity, but understanding. Texting has never, and never will be a good way of communicating when an argument is concerned. No matter your intention, tone or diction, it is ultimately determined by those who receive it. Depending on their current mood, they can easily misinterpret it.

As Marshall, McLuhan, the Canadian philosopher renowned for his studies on the effect mass-media and audience thought and behaviour, famously said;

> "The medium is the message. How you say things is more important than what you say".

Fear of Talking on the Phone

Despite it being similar to texting in that it acts as a safety barrier between you and the other, it seems the thought of picking up the phone has an even greater hold on our levels of anxiety and worry. To have a fear for conversing indicates, in reality, the fear of the person and his/her response, and the unknown outcome. Therefore, you have to take command of your space, with everything needing to abide by your rules and standards in order to pass. Remember, if you are anxious about making the first move, then you are attached to the result. Lose attachment to it by first establishing your intentions on your end, and the fear of whatever is on the other side will be diluted into non-existence.

Referring back to the chapter on making a decision, if you are to make a phone call, but are about to do so from a worried, overwhelmed or angry mindset, then don't. Let the situation, opportunity, and space come back to you. You should only make a call when you are in your best frame of self.

Try this the next time you have to make a call or are about to receive one. This is where thinking forward can actually act as the solution. Imagine the other person on the side. Have a picture of them clear in your mind. It doesn't matter if you don't know what they look like (say it is a cold call). Now, as the phone is ringing, envision them noticing, moving over, then finally picking it up. By having this scenario to focus your thoughts on, it is almost like you are actually having a face-to-face conversation, with all the negative energy that once existed now lost in the air of conversation. Again, having a moment to sit in your own space and be affirmative in where you are, will allow for you to consciously take hold and repel any anxiety that comes with. Remember, **it is not the other person you are afraid of, but the space between you**. Gradually, you will ease your way out of texting, and find yourself faced with the opportunity to use the phone. Soon, the phone will become a more prominent, direct way you will naturally want to communicate.

Note: Outside the window, as I am editing this chapter, there is a man speaking on the phone. I have no idea what he is saying, yet his passion when he talks invites fascination. Hand gestures, pointing adamantly as if he is speaking down the phone directly to his recipient. It is like he no longer aware they are on the phone, but joined together by a space two worlds apart.

Networking: Detaching from Others

Once the prevalent role that artificial communication played in my life had diminished, I slowly began to open up the shell that I had unknowingly trapped myself in. What followed was the unexpected feeling of complete openness, and more so, the unparalleled path of opportunity. Although I did not know it at first, this was the true way of networking that I had been longing for.

In his section on detachment, Dyer highlights that "Networking acts as a great way to detach. Especially from people".

At first, I was quite unaware what this truly meant in regards to people. However, as I became more involved in the process of putting first things first, and gaining the momentum that evaded me before, I realised how much networking aids in the art of letting the situation dictate the outcome between those you meet.

Rather than going into a conversation with someone expecting a certain outcome. Talk to people. Get to know their interests; what they do, who they know, where they got their skills. These are people with whom you can share interests and learn from. Comparing each other's skill and limitations while expanding your own knowledge, rather than expecting something, or seeing them, as for what they can give you. I found the more time I spent with people, without judgement, the more avenues unexpectedly opened. I was interested in this one thing, and it turned out they had a connection with someone that provided this opportunity and so on.

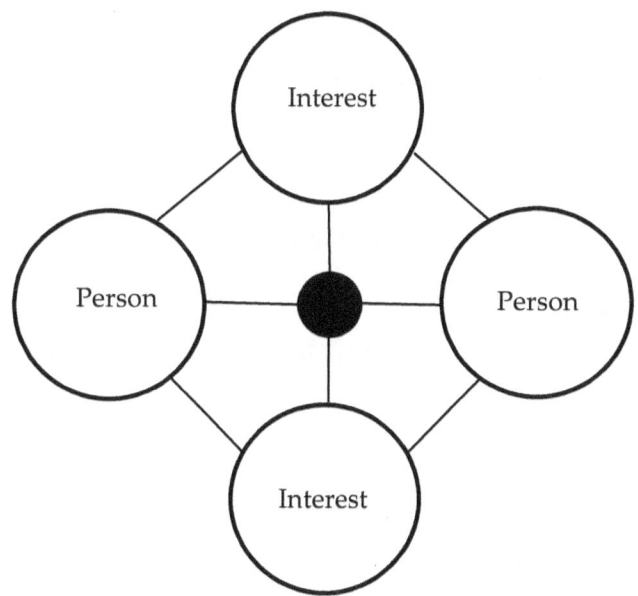

Taking This Further

I was once asked by my father, to write a short paragraph titled *What is culture?* In it, I observed through the practices and functions of my own sporting groups and friends, the strengths, weaknesses and limits that cause the lifespan of a culture to either flourish or decay.

A strength of new cultures, is that in this innocence of new existence, they are able to assess what works, what doesn't, and then decide what they need to add of their own that strengthen the overall essence of the club. However, without a common goal to bind people together, with rituals, routine, principles and practice, it won't last beyond simple existing. Using age as an example, I made the point that while older people have experience, (role of tribal elders) and serve as the foundation, youth is where evolution happens. **Vitality brings versatility, and versatility brings variety.**

Any aspiring culture (or in this case network) must have a combination of both young and old, but not to the extent where there is a 'leader' controlling and dictating, but instead a mentor connected and directing responsibility down the chain. Open to ideas, values and methods. When working in a group, consider the skill level of each individual's area of expertise, and revise it for a practical, realistic setting (what you have at your disposal). Often, when we are leading (I have been guilty of this), we become overprotective of our power, and thus lose sight of the vision in our overattachment. It is not about your vision, but bringing the overall one to fruition.

As you will learn later in *Pathways: College, Job, Career*, don't think of it as having to climb a ladder, a set path to follow, rather expanding your level off knowledge through a bridge of differences in the context of experience. Networking is that bridge. Ultimately, it is not just about group, divisions or rankings, as separate entities, but the entire amalgamation of a culture's overall potential. The group's potential is dependent on having members who are willing to ascend to that level.

Skill without 'will' is systematic killing. Division of differences creates divide, while vision with differences, create harmony.

By having a web of connections which naturally allows to connect with people through your common interests, you immediately halve the work load of pressure you inflict unnecessarily. We feel have to do it all on our own. This is simply not true. There are millions of people just like you out there. Surround yourself with people who share the same interests, goals, and ambitions. It is very much a symbiotic relationship of equitably equal contribution. A partnership of giving and receiving. The student helping teacher until the roles are interchangeable.

Interestingly, this refers back to the model of one thing affecting everything, (what you think is of most importance). The line is not vertical, there is no one tower of greater importance than the other, but rather that the foundation spreads further, expands its territory wider. Its reach and thus value is far more than any skyscraper that towers upwards.

<u>Physical Health:</u>
<u>Mental Awareness to Transform Your Outer Image</u>

During my final years of high school, I was constantly reminded of my body and the way it looked. "Boy, your legs are skinny. They look like twigs". It was as if I too were noticing it for the first time myself. I would also get comments like; "You need to eat more", as if it were necessary to be acceptable in their eyes. Now, technically, they were right. Eating more and gaining weight would benefit me in many ways, however it is easy to say this, without understanding how difficult it was for me (born so early with a monstrous metabolism) to do so.

Hearing phrases like these deeply affected my confidence, and ultimately because others saw me that way, I too felt the way I looked was not good enough. There was one moment in particular where things reached a turning point. I was performing at an Election Drama Entertainment Night in my senior year at high school. An acquaintance of mine, who was in the year below also performing. After my act had finished, I came across her backstage. The first words that came from her mouth was, not; "Oh good performance

Justin", not, "you were great", but the same fateful phrase I had heard so many times before. "You are so skinny!" Yes, I know black is a slimming colour, but wow.

It was in that moment I decided I wanted to change my body. I needed to. I was sick and tired of having this be the defining factor for how I was seen by others, and how I made myself feel. However, after years of going through the repetitive process to make this change, (implementing an exercise routine only for it to slip away into obscurity), I still had no control over my body. Something was missing, and although I did not realise, it was adherently clear every time. You don't even have to look in the mirror to remind yourself. It is just there, and deep down you know it is a part of yourself that you should fix. Not because people tell you to, but because it is physically possible to.

In order for you to have control over what you want to change you must first understand it.

Disclaimer: There will be no pre-designed workouts or diet plans to follow. Everyone reading is coming from diverse range physiques with different bodily needs and goals. Depending on your starting point, you will have distinct ways your body will react to certain types of training. As discussed in the process of self-learning chapter, it is important to work the student around the teachings. The last thing I want is to give you a routine, with promises that this is the golden 'one size fits all' ticket. It will be much more beneficial to the understanding of your own body, if you go out, and actively research, test, and reflect. I AM NOT A LISCENED

PROFESSIONAL. Any concerns regarding your practices should be discussed with your doctor, physician or any other healthcare provider prior to and/or during.

Your Ideal Physique: A Three-Dimensional Body

Stand right now in front of your mirror and assess your figure. Be totally and truly honest with yourself. What exactly is it about yourself you want to change?

For me, it sounded simple. I wanted to gain weight.

We make the mistake in our honesty, by being too vague, saying, "I want to put on weight, or lose it". This is ultimately true, but the process that holds this together is much more in-depth. One of the leading reasons why I would fail in my attempts was that I would get too focused on the end result, without actually defining what my goals were (obviously a product of my forward thinking). With every exercise came a higher expectation that it had to have immediate see-able results. We have this grand picture in our head of what we should look like and become overwhelmed by the pressure, as we have not set both distinct goals and reasons for these goals.

We need to simplify our thinking. Be detailed by being specific, and specific by being detailed. I'll ask you again. This time, from another angle. **Why** do you want to lose/gain weight?

> To fit into my clothes. F.I.T. (Fit into T-shirt)
> For people to stop commenting on my figure.
> To feel confident and complete when I look in the mirror.
> To fix my posture and any other ailments and pains.

> Improve my overall level of fitness and strength (sick of feeling under breath and exhausted).
> To look like those in the magazines so I can be successful.

That last one was a test. From pictures in magazines, to actors and actresses in television and film, multimedia dictates the way we should look according to societies' standards of beauty. We start to compare to ourselves to others, with a physique anything less than that standard is deemed unacceptable. That is the one thing I can pride myself on. I never once felt the need to compare myself to others or societal standards. I knew that this would only cause false expectations, ones that ultimately, I could never reach. Remember the analogy of uniting alphas and betas. Use a successful physique of another as an inspirational guideline.

ULTIMATE PRINCIPLE: **Do not compare yourself to others.**

With that said, now record yourself standing in front of a camera. About two or three meters away. **What** exactly is it about your body that you want to change?

Perhaps you want to look wider, or thinner. Where? Your arms? Legs? Hips? Waist? Shoulders? Now turn to the side. We do not want to just look good in the mirror or picture. Light, angles and your mental pride all play a factor in what makes a photograph appealing. We want something less one-dimensional, and a physique that is more wholesome from all sides. Proportionate to your bone structure, limb to torso length, and over body shape. One that matches our honest self. Based on true intention. A body that completes the totality within you.

Factors That Stop Us from Initiating This Change: Self-Consciousness & Environment

Although is very easy to affirm oneself that it is the right thing to do to transform their body, as soon as we are faced with the prospect of others watching or being involved with that process; we become more self-conscious than ever. It's a paradox where we like the privacy of their own space (free of judgement), yet have no direction as to what exactly we need to practice.

For countless years I worked out in an old shed that was uneven, dusty, cramp, and open to the scorching sun. I focused all my attention on the negative aspects of this environment, instead of where it should have been, the moment of the exercise. You need an environment that is spacious, easy to move in, and where you can transition from exercise to exercise with minimal effort and time wasted. This is the major strength of going to a conventional gym, however note that you are not just dealing with yourself and your workout, but countless others. It can sometimes be hard to keep a set routine when you are competing for equipment or space. I knew this going in, and thus was my reasoning to primarily exercise alone. However sooner or later, I had to address the possibility whether it was hiding a genuine emotion. Fear.

If you are too nervous about going to a public gym, you have two choices;

1) Create a home gym to workout in.

2) Suck it up and go to the gym.

Nobody really cares about the skinny or fat person at the gym. They are too preoccupied and focused on themselves to have time to care, and if they do, they are jealous of the fact you are putting in the hard work to make a change, something they don't have to do. And if they do look, it will only be for an instant, then they will move on. If that still doesn't convince you. That's okay. It's a process, you can build your way up to that. Start out at home to gain that bit of self-confidence. Gyms and environments where multiple people and group classes are available will become a great way for networking alongside people with common interests. The benefits will become available when you yourself become available.

You cannot change your exterior without first changing your interior outlook.

Lack of Knowledge: What Approach Should I Take?

There are so many types of exercises and terms that go along with the art of fitness and general health. Whether it be bodybuilding, powerlifting, calisthenics, cross-fit or aerobics, it can be quite overwhelming for the novice individual to even begin to understanding which approach is the best. Now obviously, this will be determined by what your goal is and what your body needs, however a fatal mistake we make is when having a goal that is too vague, we bring with it a lack of knowledge that is detrimental to setting our foundation.

If you want to primarily gain or lose weight, then do exercises that are specifically designed to do that. I was once, like you are probably now, one of those people at the gym wandering aimlessly around with no direction or idea of what it is we should be doing. The common mantras are if you want to **gain** weight/muscle, eat more than you are moving (eat big/lift heavy), and if you want to **lose** weight, move more than you are eating (eat less/move more). This is, when you simplify it, absolutely true, however when you actually get to doing this, there is such a lengthy process of the 'doing' which causes great confusion. Our choice of exercise and 'style' is going to depend on two things. The initial starting point of your body, and the limit of your metabolism, muscle length, and bone structure. For example, my legs are long and lean. If I wanted to build them, I would have to prioritise my attention towards weight training. Not running. Now, for someone's who were thick and heavy (perhaps this extends to the entire body), and therefore wanted to lose the fat around them, running would be appropriate to start.

Now assess your body, in terms of **functionality**. Perhaps your abdominals are weak/or covered by a large layer of fat. It is therefore evident that you should focus on exercises that strengthen/target that area. Maybe you are able to perform lunges, but are weaker on one side than the other. Your focus should be perfecting this movement. Start on the level that you can according to **your current fitness level.** You can't be expected to do a high-intensity workout when you can't even walk. Going back to having a goal for each body part, choose an area that you would like to change (say arms or legs), and then exercises you can do to target that. Whether you do this by utilising **compound movements**, meaning using your entire body, or the **isolation** of a single muscle, take that time before you start this journey to assess your abilities and limitations. It will not only make your efforts that much less stressful, but cause you to less likely drop out before you leave the starting line.

Excess Knowledge

On the flip side, the other mistake we make is that in trying to understand our body's needs, we take in more information than we can, and should handle. In this world full of online content, we can easily get consumed with making sure we do things right. A common occurrence that plagued my efforts, was that I and would not feel it in the area that the task was designed for. This also created an additional problem where I would focus on the fact that it wasn't working, and all my frustration and worry to desperately fix it would stop me from actually focusing on the movement.

The first step I would advise is to perform the exercise as you initially think it should be performed, just by off pure instinct. Then take note of these two things;

A) Are you feeling it in the correct areas?

B) Is there pain in areas where there are not supposed to be?

If you are feeling A) Keep doing it. If B) Then that is telling you need to (as shown in the process of self-learning chapter), research. If you don't know. Ask. In regards to the beginning of any physical transformation (especially weight training), the first few weeks are most important. They should be focused on two things.

1. Learning the correct form of each exercise.
2. Becoming aware to how your body should properly function in conjunction with this from.

The goal here is to make sure you are feeling the muscles that you want to grow/firm up contracting, whilst giving your body the experience of moving dynamically against or with a set force. To be stimulated.

Every effective relationship is built on communication, and through consistency, you are communicating to your body that you want your body to adapt. I recommend starting off using light weights (or bodyweight), enough for the muscles to feel what the correct form is like. Respect the movement and feel the form. It is easier to create a good habit, than work all the way back to change a bad one.

By working out every single day in these initial weeks, you create discipline through consistency (also what is known as muscle memory patterns or habits). Once they are engrained into your subconscious, you do not think about them anymore. They set the foundation for everything that is to follow. This is why I believe at its core, why myself and so many others fail to transform their body. They have not done the work to stop and really listen to their body. What it needs in relation to how it currently functions. Many workout forums ask you to take note of your workout and every exercise; the number of times you repeat it. If you are a beginner, this will only overwhelm you. Your focus should be on acting in the moment. I found that rather than obsessing over this at first, start with a summary of each workout. Firstly, what exercises you did and the weight used. Then, what you feel worked and what did not. Lastly, what you need to work on for next time. Each time, the list will get smaller and smaller, giving positive feedback and reassuring you are doing things right. By constantly associating yourself with these bad things, you can never get to a place a total relaxation and focus.

To get into the flow of a workout, do exercises that you know work, and leave the ones you are struggling with till last. Don't force yourself to do it doesn't feel right. **Have a relationship with your body.** By that, treat each session as active meditation and let it communicate to you throughout. Some days you will feel like you are too sore, that you might injure yourself. Others, that you need to train at a higher intensity. Once I came to the epiphany that my quest wasn't to change my body, but to gain a deeper understanding and relationship with it, results started to happen.

What If I Lose Interest and Focus?

The intent and mindset are just as, if not more important than the task itself. By taking that initiative to make that change, you are already on the right track, but what happens when that track just stops? What happens when you just can't find that motivation and feeling that was propelling you forward?

Going back to the chapter on lack of motivation and excitement, this means that you have become too comfortable in your situation. An issue that presents itself to those who have had multiple failed attempts at transforming your body, is that even though we may have an understanding of what our body needs, and how it works, we have no idea how to evolve into a higher state when our efforts lack results. One of the negative things about a routine that has been implemented for a while, is that your body becomes accustomed to the methods you have been using thus far. When the moment of plateauing comes, this is a sign you need to (as discussed before), flip the script. Remember the process of self-learning. Building up. Breaking down. Simplifying. Repeat.

This is where the different training structures, and perspectives come back into play. By delving into other training styles, you are able to broaden your options and possibilities for results. This comes with experimentation, but as long as you go into it with full openness and no judgement, you will surprise yourself. With each outlook comes a different way to understanding your body. Take what works for you, the essence from each and discard what doesn't. Be it weight training (strength/hypertrophy), boxing/skipping (high-intensity), or walking/running and swimming. Although seemingly different in approach and effect, the common interest is having a different way to express and understand the human body. Ultimately, it is this in conjunction with your lifestyle and outlook into why you are doing this that determines how your physique looks and comes across. Once more, it is an extension of your true self internally projected outward. The living embodiment of the totality that is you.

Note: Sometimes it is necessary to take a break from the quest altogether. Often, when things were not feeling right, I would take a period of one to three weeks off to reset and asses everything; training, diet, etc. It is amazing how returning after a hiatus unlocks a new perspective.

Don't feel like you have to constantly force yourself at the expense of your overall well-being. There is a difference between forcing out of laziness, and out of weariness.

What If I Am Still Not Seeing Results?

For years on end, my numbers on the scale would go up, yet, I wouldn't see, or feel any notable change. It was if no matter the diversity of my efforts, I was always doomed to stay in this state I had been assigned to a birth. When that girl said the words; "You are so skinny", it lit a fire inside me. A fire that while had the flames of motivation, was still based on embers of bitterness. I then referred myself back to the chapter on addiction, and more specially, the idea of identifying my attempts as a battle. I realised then and there, I was doing the same thing here, only this time, driven by the need to succeed. I believe the ability to not only keeping consistent with a routine, but achieving an honest body is embedded in a something that is severely misinterpreted by most.

Accepting your current form.

When offered as a suggestion by others that we should consider transforming our body, we often make the excuse (really it is just us acting in denial) it is too hard, and something they could never see themselves doing. So, we say "oh I'm fine as I am. You should accept who you are no matter what shape". This is correct, but it's coming from a state a denial, laziness and doubt. It is hard. It takes time. That is the point. It is this ordinance that is a defining factor in your lack of success. Go back to the principle on page 198, then 26. There are countless people out there who have all the reason in the world to complain, but don't. In their misfortune, they have accepted their form, to the point where is no longer a detriment, but a power. You should do the same. It would be an insult to their willpower not to.

You must be able to accept your current form, to reach your ideal one. The qualities you possess still exist no matter what package they come in. This concept is something that will be a reoccurring aspect that you will have to reintroduce throughout your journey. Some days, you will feel like you hate your body. That is okay. It does not matter whether your body is lighter or heavier than it was yesterday. Your exterior form is exactly that where it needs to be to in order to catch up to your interior spirit. It all a part of the process.

It's more what the body says about you. A full representation of your best assets. For you. Not for others to say about you.

Which is easier? To lose weight or gain it? Those say it is the heavier person as they have the weight to lose, while the lighter person has to create their mass. From the other perspective, it may seem veritable, though, it is actually irrelevant. They both require hard work methods according to their own body, and how it reacts to certain types of training. What is more important is what person is behind the body.

Pathways: Job, College, Career

Cast your mind back to the chapter on *The Process of Self-Learning*. Towards the end I touched on whether formal study was necessary? Something that I came across after completing my degree in communications (majoring in media production) was a scene from the film, *The Secret of My Success*, starring Michael J. Fox and directed by Herbert Ross. In it, his character has just moved from the small country town to fulfill his dreams in the big city. After receiving a call back for an interview, he sits face to face with the man in charge of personnel development (played by Jack Dalton). This is how it unfolded.

<u>Dalton</u>

I'm sorry Mr. Foster we need someone with experience.

<u>Fox</u>

But how can I get any experience until I get a job that gives me experience?

<u>Dalton</u>

If we gave you a job just to give you experience, you'd take that experience and get a better job, and that experience would benefit someone else.

<u>Fox</u>

Yeah, but I was trained in college to handle a job like this. So, in a sense I already have experience.

<u>Dalton</u>

What you've got is college experience. Not the practical hard-nosed business experience we are looking for. Had you joined our training program out of high school you'd be qualified for this job now.

<u>Fox</u>

Then why did I go to college?

<u>Dalton</u>

Had fun, didn't you?

Well... If, I personally had a chance to respond. No, not really.

Upon graduating high school, decided I wanted to go into the film industry. Having always been interested in fantasy, dreams, and writing stories as a child, it hit me one day, if they can do it, why can't I? As wide eyed as we are that time in our life, those goals still hold great value. Most constantly find it a struggle to find out what they want to do, for a career, so I considered myself lucky for that reason, getting a rush of excitement and belief in myself that had been working against me my entire high school experience. So, I, like many, looked towards the most obvious option to go study at film school. It was the practical side of study was what I was most drawn to. However, there were many other thoughts going through my mind.

- It was expensive.
- It was two hours travel away both ways.
- It was basically what everyone else was doing. I wanted to set myself apart.

I asked my parents to pitch to me their perspective. They too expressed their concern for the many problems that I would be likely to face. They also said it was crucial to have a backup plan in case things did not turn out the way you had hoped for, as the industry was extremely competitive. When they studied at university, it was provided to them without expense by the government, so there was no real reason not to. It was just societal norm to go from school, college, and then out into the workforce. Sure, you had people who would take a year off to travel, but I knew the way I would approach it, if I were to break off from formal structured learning, I would be inclined not to come back. Simply put, I wanted it over and done with.

Four years later, and forty thousand dollars' worth in student debt (I know that is considerably inexpensive compared to most countries), I had no real understanding in my field or the confidence to go out and pursue something. You ask what is even the point?

My first ever class of university was one that I vividly remember. A compact room with two-by-two desks parallel to its walls, the tutor laid casually on his own. All eager to learn the great teachings that this higher form of learning had to offer, I waited for his first opening line.

"Can someone tell me what the point of school was?"

We all sat in silence, looking around for the other to make the first suggestion.

"To learn?", one said.

"To grow?"

"No", said the tutor. "Try again".

Lastly, a friend of mine, who was a few years older and had studied before, put up his hand.

"To sit down, shut up and follow rules".

"Correct".

I sat with this for a moment. Well, in essence, it is true. You are required to follow a routine, wear a particular uniform, and complete work within a set period of time. This system is to prepare you for the bigger structure of work life. Formal study isn't meant for play time. It is an institution designed to bring up people with skills for the workplace to contribute to active society. Now we absolutely need this, as without we wouldn't have qualified doctors, engineers, lawyers, financiers, scientists and so on, but as an experience itself, I personally was not really in the right mindset to approach and process the information given to me.

Now referring back to the chapter on self-learning, you can argue that this is entirely my fault. Now, to a degree, it is understandable why it is it can be seen that way, but I was being taught these topics, going to all these lectures, buying all these textbooks, reading chapter after chapter of prescribed readings, but with no real practical relevance to follow up on how this might relate to something on the job. I had to do all that self-realisation on my own, with no understanding of how to get there.

As a result, once I graduated, I struggled to apply for a job where my skills were applicable and I could see myself doing. Everything that I had built up in my mind now felt so out of grasp. No longer was there a safety net around me. This was the big wide world, and I did not feel prepared at all. All the jobs in this industry were geared towards the direction of social media (you know how I feel about that). Furthermore, they were all situated in an office environment, something I knew I would grow tiresome of very quickly. The path was no longer clear and now I was just like everyone out there with a piece of paper and with no authentic experience, when (just like in the movie), that is exactly what I needed. So, I shutdown, returning to a space of defeat and comfort. I did not work for an entire year, only supporting by my weekend job I got through college. The year passed, and I was back where I started. I knew I had to get more of an income. I was persuaded by my parents to go on welfare to assist me in finding a job.

I had to apply for twenty jobs and month, plus go to appointments every fortnight to receive my benefits. This proved more difficult than it seemed. Although I had a qualification, there was nothing relevant that they could provide me with. I was over-qualified. The only jobs they had going for were for kitchen hands, cleaning roles, call centres and factory lines. Now after spending four years of your time at university, working jobs like these were the last thing on my mind. Yet it was my only option. See *

The 9 to 5 Structure

After going to the interview and being accepted on an unpaid monthly internship, I began the monotonous task of the nine to five. Just as people can become consumed by unpleasant habits, toxic relationships, and addictions, people can be consumed by their work environment. It suffocates all the surrounding energy and restricts any possibility for creative flow. A repetitive structure combined with a terrible working environment is a leading factor in creating anxiety, and serves as the foundation for destructive habits to flourish. From personal experience, with this constant routine, I would finish at 5:00, sometimes 5:30 if I stayed over-time, to get home around 6:00. By the time I had a shower, cooked dinner and settled down, I had no energy or motivation to do anything productive. Like the welfare system, I was locked in by a contract with this office job. I felt extremely trapped within what was meant to be my life! It did not matter if I was depressed, or exhausted, or abused, I had to work to earn a living. Now there is a fine line between sucking it up and working hard for a purpose, and just working.

> *"At work it is not what you made today, but what you were made into. Not just what you produced, but what is being produced in you".* - John Scherer

Note: These structures of work are all dependant on your priorities. Of course, if you have a family and need to support children, you will need a secure occupation to match.

A Casual Job/Part-time

Now you can't just quit your main source of income and live off good intentions. The idea is that you are using this job to give you more time to work towards a better one. Whilst actively working on yourself, you are researching possible avenues and opportunities. An opportunity provides an experience. The experience provides training in the different working environments one might come across, as well as the varied structure and people dynamics involved within each. A casual/part-time job, whilst temporary, will help you reset your bearings and breathe a breath of fresh air into your life. In saying this, you will need one that is not too taxing and gives you ample time to pursue your main goal. Now, of course if you are living by yourself, this is much easier than if you have a pre-existing commitment to a family. Just as one thing affects everything, you will have to balance your life in such a way where the trade-offs are at a minimum.

After this ordeal, I did not want to fall back into the scenario where I so desperately needed out of. I applied for a position at a book factory close to where I lived. Instead of 9:00 to 5:00, it was 6:30 to 2:00, and almost $10 more than my job as a designer. Furthermore, the work itself was the complete opposite to the office. On your feet instead of sitting, morning and lunch break as opposed to one, and the freedom to talk and work at the same time compared to constantly walking on eggshells. Why didn't I start this sooner? People often feel obligated to their employees to stay, regardless of the negative effects it may have on themselves. They are often too scared and hesitant to make that final step in putting forward a decision. All because of a guilty conscious. Quitting is sometimes necessary so you can take a step back, evaluate your path then look to move forward. Be realistic though.

With this new structure, the freedom and time I had gained lifted a substantial weight of my shoulders. I could start work early and finish with the entire afternoon left to me to relax and complete tasks that were actively contributing towards my betterment. No longer was I coming home mentally, emotionally and physically drained, ready to indulge in my addictions to cope.

It was during this period that I came across my grandmother's coffee table that started it all. Utilizing my lunch breaks to write the first notes of what would become this book, I still had the dream swirling in my subconscious. Deep down I knew it was something I had to venture forth with all the way.

* Never look down on someone for doing these types of jobs. Someone has to do them, and at some stage in your life you may have to. With so many people unemployed, homeless or in dire need of income, it is ignorant (unless absolutely necessary) to turn a blind eye to them. It is a necessary part of experiencing the realities of the workforce. Treat people like these as if you would your boss. With respect. The difference is that these people at the 'bottom' of the totem pole have a reason for acting sour, your boss on the other hand, should have no reason to be.

The Perception of Our Path

In my final year of university, I took a mandatory class on discourse in the media. The tutor was a casual whom I had not seen my entire tertiary career. After years of dry, lifeless, teachers who seemed less enthused than the students, it was like a new life-force had been presented to me. She would explain, and explain again, giving reference to how it related to the outside world. Whether it be through, diagrams or videos, she would make sure everyone understood, and didn't continue until we were all on the same page. Being the end of term, the class attendance rate had been more than halved, (with me the adept student I was), showing up along with a handle of others. Ironically, it is not the content of the class itself that I remember. In hindsight, it is irrelevant. Rather, it is the last conversation that this tutor had to bring things full circle.,

"Does anyone think about where they are going, their path and what may be as a result of things?"

The class remained silent.

"I do. All the time", replied. "I think it is important to know where you are going. To consider your options, whether or not your path is right. I'm always in that process of expanding, seeing what works, and why things don't and trying to find my place in it all". "Good", the tutor replied, a warm expression appearing on her face.

With that my final experience of tertial education was over. I thanked my teacher for her wise words throughout the semester, telling her how much I appreciated and related to it, and left. Comparing this last day to my first day, do I regret it? Well, it depends. On one hand, I am grateful I had the experience. It was a definite path I took, where I met and lost many people. On the other, did I really learn anything? About myself or my selected career field? I know not everyone's situation is the same as mine, and depending on your habitus and situation, it may be absolutely crucial to study formally. I now realise that learning is different to understanding. Although I can't redo my college experience, I can give you my thoughts into what I should have done **on top** of this study.

Options If You Don't Study

In the words of my father, "You can do one of three philosophies. Use your brains, brawn or beauty. Blue Collar. Red Collar. White Collar". Depending on if the field you want to get into requires a degree for qualification, you should do absolutely do formal study. It provides a safe and secure environment and a clear pathway and direction for years. However, regardless of your decision I would strongly advise to have multiple avenues to further your options.

These include:

1. Work experience 2. Internships 3. Volunteering

There are an exponential range of resources out there that are available to you regardless if you were formally studying. Public libraries. Books. The internet. Articles. Other people. All knowledge is self-knowledge. Apart from the formal exams, how much of the content that you are learning, can be learnt on your own time from the comfort of your own space? This secondary source can only get you so far though. You need practical primary experience of putting this knowledge into action.

- Ask yourself what you would enjoy doing for a living.
- Acquire an in-depth knowledge of your passion.
- Research the different avenues (options and pathways) to get a foot in the door.

All these, I believe are much easier if you ask, inquire and research the aspects of **yourself first.** By this I mean;

 - Clear communicative skills.

 - Calm demeanour and able to handle confrontations

 - Competent reading and writing

 - Able to express your ideas vividly

Having something to say. What do you want to contribute to the world? What part of yourself do you want to express? This goes in part with the chapter on having multiple interests. Refer to the process of self-learning.

Process. Tools. Craft.

Licenses

There are also many licenses you can acquire to give you boarder skills and options.

- Vehicle Licenses
- Green cards
- White Cards
- RSA/RCG (able to serve alcohol and gambling services)
- An apprenticeship or a trade.
- Short courses at community colleges/Tafes. These provide a more practical approach with first-hand experience relevant to your industry. Perhaps it would be beneficial (where relevant) for more tertiary colleges to construct their more literate courses in collaboration with practical courses.

Going back to the scene at the beginning of this chapter. When Fox's character does eventually receive a job at the start of the second act, he is met with this following remark.

Interviewer

Well, what impresses me most is the amount of experience you picked up while still attending college.

Fox

Well Ma'am, I knew all those years at college would be worthless without practical hard-nosed business experience.

Although this is done in jest for the sake for the scene, it is true.

Two Birds With One Purpose

We are often asked what we want to do for a living. I feel the better question is how do we want to structure it? What do I mean by structure? Well, like I said in the chapter of structured perspective, ask yourself how do you want your house (life) to be built? What foundations are you building it on? This whole book has been designed to rebuild your foundation. Now, you need to find the structure in order to reach the steeple. We all want the freedom to work when we want and not feel locked into an unmalleable system by someone else commanding us. In order to do this, you have to use your time to put other things into motion.

For example; let us say you can fit all your classes into two days of your week. Then you use the rest of the days for an internship, work experience and a casual job. Then use your weekend for either sport, study, or weekend work. Even if half of the day is broken up into an internship/work experience, and the rest if used for an afternoon/night job, then so be it. If this clashes with other aspects of your schedule, then perhaps you need to review your current lifestyle, and question whether you should be balancing out your commitments to other areas. I understand, for most, this will be quite a mammoth task. You may have others dependant on you (children), but rather than seeing this as a burden, take it as a test to simply your life to the most functional way possible

We study to work, work to live and live to work.

We should have the ambition and determination, to turn this statement around.

We work to study, study to live and live to live.

Remember what I alluded to in regards to addressing what is most accessible to your current situation? Absolutely, our mindset is most in our control, but in contrast, how much of this is influenced by our environment? If your situation is causing you this much repetitive anxiety, it may be that you need to first move out of this environment. What does this require though?

First, a reason. A new occupation. This then, may require a degree to provide wider opportunities. This sacrifices time and requires commitment, something that needs an income while you complete this ongoing task. A nine to five structure, although consistent in job security and pay, gives little leeway of time, and more open to stress. A casual job with more freedom, but less pay. It's up to you to decide what is needed for you in this moment. You can always start out, like I did, with full-time work for a year or two, and ease up once settled, to something more casual. Soon you will then be ready to venture forth with your individual goal. I remember back on my time at the job agency. There were people who would not settle for anything less than the high-end job they had in their mind.

One man in particular, was adamant he deserved a job at a high-end real-estate agency, as that is what he had prior experience in. Yet instead of settling for a lesser-known agency as a start, he complained for what was available to him. Sure, he may have these skills, but the way he was delegating around the issue, you could see that was not his only problem that needed sorting.

Budgeting Your Expenses

We work to live, and live to work, and all the time we seem only to just get by. This endless cycle of survival can be extremely problematic when you are trying to put the things you have learnt into action, yet all the while worrying about where the next pay check will come from. By calculating your weekly and monthly expenses, you can differentiate between what you need and what you can go without. The idea is that if you can take a day or two off, this day can then break up your week, relieve stress, are more importantly, provide time to do tasks that contribute towards your goal. Use this following table to calculate the amount you as an **individual** would have left after your fortnightly earnings. If you are a couple who both earn an income, then this will obviously be doubled.

	Weekly	Biweekly	Monthly
Rent/Utilities			
Food			
Fuel			
Total			

You may think this is being frugal. That this is designed as if you were to live off the bare minimum. That is the point. Once I actually sat down and realised where I was spending my expenses, I discovered that all the stress I was having with money, could be cut in half by simply revaluating my priorities with I actually needed to survive. All the nights out. The takeaway. Sure, it can be rewarding sometimes, but if done regularly, it all adds up over the course of the week, and then month.

Some More Things to Consider:

> Of course, there are other expenses that are accumulated monthly, such as car insurance, water/electrics, phone bills etc, but the same principles apply. Don't forgot all the needless subscriptions you may have forgotten about. Magazines. Online accounts. Gym memberships.

> Debt: This is your priority if you have any. Credit cards, electrical/water bills, fines, car insurance, etc. These will leave an enormous burden on yourself if left unchecked. The phrase, 'this will set you back', becomes apparent with you realise how much momentum you have lost from endless spending, and how much work is then needed to climb back out.

> Going through your wardrobe and storing only what you wear is a practical way to cut down on the endless spending of items. Clothes that once worn, will only then be locked away. Sell the good stuff and donate the rest to charity. This goes for any furniture, or jewellery, you aren't attached to. Items that sit alone gathering dust instead of being utilized.

>Start buying more at thrift stores. You are helping the smaller charities and supporting those who need it more than you.

>Consider working on the weekends to earn extra pay from the weekend rate.

> By structuring your diet, you can decide what essential you need, and dispose of all the unessentials **you think** you need. Snacking is a habit, that messes up any diet through inconsistent eating. Create

a meal plan with easy to prepare options. Cooking in itself, is another positive task associated with the true-self.

Visualize this;

There is a homeless person in the city. Hundreds of thousands of people pass by them during the course of a day. There can be no doubt that every single one of those people, have a dollar hidden away in their wallet. Let's say ten people gave that person their dollar. That could mean a hot meal for breakfast.

How about twenty people? That could be the equivalent of both lunch and dinner. If fifty people gave away their dollar, that could be food for the week. Perhaps even a fresh shirt. What if one hundred people parted ways their hard-earned dollar?

That could mean accommodation for the night, and a shower for the morning. Extend this to two hundred. Five hundred. A thousand. These people have close to nothing, yet all it takes is a glimpse of kindness to reassure them they still have everything to live for. I guarantee you that all these people walking past, weren't even aware the dollar was there in the first place. I always carry a few spare coins with me when out. Those few (depending on whom I give it to) could mean the difference between being out of the cold, and in a warm bed.

Remember, there is always someone worse off than you.

Crafting Your Own Career

Upon the final stretch of editing this book together, I was faced with an untimely decision that saw the work I had done come under potential jeopardy. Having been 'let go' from my job, I was being pressured to be involved with another employment agency. It was as if time was repeating itself. I could see the cycle coming round again. Envisioning the prospects of having no control or say, I became increasingly torn by, not only myself, but my family to go down this distinct path.

Then and there, I made a decision that shaped the events of everything to follow. To go forth with getting this book published at all costs. To move from the endless back and forth of dead-end occupations, to the continuous evolution of a career. While budgeting my expenses to live off my savings, I gained the freedom that allowed me to put all my attention into shaping the base for my own-self. As well as finishing the numerous drafts needed to complete a manuscript, I utilised my time crafting promotional material (business cards) and researching publishers that would be most suited to the overall message I had to say. I consumed myself in this task, to the point where it had become my full-time job.

Now of course you may not have the same aspirations as me, and may be in a different point of your journey, but what is important to read between where this can apply to your career. That's right. Life is in itself, a career. That doesn't mean do something as drastic as me, but what I am referring to is reaching a state of formality where you can create a sense of identity where it has something to say.

Resume & Cover Letter

Take the practice of assembling a resume and cover letter. Write down (on paper) all the things that initially come to your head, that are relevant to the job, things you can improve, and where your insight may apply. Don't just stock standardly state what they want to hear. Have an opinion. It is much more than protocol to communicate to an employee. It is an expression of yourself as much it is a list of requirements.

It is not you selling yourself to the employee, but the employee selling themselves to you.

They want experience in this area for x number of years, and the ability to do this and that at a certain level. Now of course, from an employee's perspective, this is absolutely reasonable, as I'm sure if you were running a business, you would want people of a specific standard to ensure you were operating at its highest ability. However, from a job seeker's perspective, there are no footholds to acquire a base to spring off from. Well, I have no experience in that, so how can I possibly be considered for this role that requires such specific criteria? Experience, we most often forget, is experience in self. The ability to;

- Be calm, collected, and work under pressure.
- Organise affairs and manage time.
- Communicate ideas and formulate strong relationships.
- A passion lined with a strong aptitude and will to learn.

I found the more I became diverse within myself, I was able to reapply to the path that I was once so afraid of venturing down. With each new inward improvement of self you master, a new outward opportunity comes available.

1. <u>Have a project that reflects your true-self.</u>

In today's multi-medium climate, there are so many platforms that you can express yourself. Design. Videography. Literature. Photography. Even statistical research. Find that specific way that allows you to be honestly yourself with minor effort. For me, this is writing. Start with this form of expression and build. You may have that end goal, the dream which is great, but rather than trying to shoot for the goal when you don't have firm control of the ball, aim for a job that gets you a base to jump off from. One of similar description, but on a smaller scale.

2. <u>Collaborate within a group. (Refer to Networking).</u>

Creatively as an entity by itself, is hard to monetise. It's marred by an extremely tight and competitive industry. By grouping your projects through a network of like-minded people (with diverse talents), not only allows for wider possibilities, but for the workload to be spread, instead of you alone. Don't be scared to extend your olive branch to those who you may actually benefit from. Perhaps those people may do the same in return.

3. <u>Develop this into a business.</u>

What skills do you have to sell? Do these skills have something that can warrant other's investment? Part of this is increasing these skills alongside your new self, to create a brand. A brand that reflects the honesty that you will put forth for others to be inspired from.

That would be my biggest piece of advice when constructing your career path. Remember genuine intention. Don't do things because everyone else as that is the prescribed way. Pinpoint specifically what it is you like about what interests you. Go down that road. Go down that road, actively, and gradually the path will reveal itself. It might not initially be the way that will work for you. Try another. One of self-expression. You will find that it is not the goal that you will be satisfied with, but the journey and the true self what made it happen. The goal is only a reflection of this. There is no one way to do something. Only the way that works for you.,

"Aim for the moon, and even if you miss, you will land amongst the stars"- Norman Vincent Peale

This phrase was repeated profusely through my last years at school, the consensus by the other students being that it was a cliche with no actual value. Now, with a deeper understanding of the reality of chasing the goal, you realise it not chasing, but constructing. How will you get to the moon? You need a rocket. How do you get a rocket? You build it.

Hopefully, this has given you an insight into how to do that.

Belief vs. Faith

There are those upon hearing the word religion, who immediately roll their eyes and scoff at the idea of there being a power above their own. The terms religion, faith and spirituality come with a great deal of stigmatism, and while religion is deeply rooted in many people's lives across a diverse range of cultures, there seems to be a great lack of knowledge or insight into how this presence relates solely to the individual. So, when it came to writing another section for this book, I was quite unsure whether or not a controversial subject such as this would even be relevant. Would my observations be received on the merit of curiosity, or be diffused simply because I mentioned the word religion? Then, I remembered a moment that happened to me that changed everything.

Tripod of Theology

It was in my first class in senior year religion, that our teacher asked us to split into three distinct groups. Those who believed, those who did not and those who weren't sure. Interestingly, as I am writing this, my mind casts back to structured perspective. The group on the left, who would classically identify themselves as atheists, were now seen as more conservative in their views. Basing their beliefs on concrete evidence (what is in front of them). Those on the right however, who were classified as conservative traditional Christian believers, were believing in a higher power above. Almost like a reversed model of the metaphor.

So, the class parted into these different perspectives, with those who didn't on the left, those who weren't sure in the middle, and lastly those who did, on the right. I for one was very confused as to my place in it all. I never went to church, only saying grace on the conventional public holidays (even then it was because I felt required to). On one hand, I was obliged to my family's beliefs, while on the other I was desperately trying to make my own conclusions. So, at the last second, I diverted from the middle (agnostic) view, to the right side of the class. Although it felt I did the right thing in that moment, there was still that sense of questioning why I made that decision. None of it was off my own contribution and understanding. It was just simply because my family were 'religious'. The discussion of these varied perspectives commenced, with those who did not believe, firmly stating that how can a deity who is almighty and powerful let all these horrific things such as disease, famine, natural disasters and death ravage the earth. The rebuttal by the right religious supporters (me excluded), insisted that it is all a part of 'God's plan'. The middle stayed out of it, expressing that they were on the fence due to a lack of empirical evidence, and absence of spiritual awareness.

Although this happened years ago, this fifteen-minute-long experience stayed with me. I may have 'chose' a 'side' to be on for that exercise, but part of me felt like I needed to be in a fourth category. Separate from it all, (much like the teacher), as if I already had the answers that transcended the noise. Noise that didn't actually bring the conversation to any real resolution or conclusion.

So, being slightly less naïve than I am now, I moved from the faith that had been prescribed to me at birth, and looked for another set of beliefs in the circle of common creeds. I came across Buddhism, because there was no 'god' or over preachiness that would push me away. Peace, love and meditation. It sounded inviting. Without judgement. When people asked me, (or through a survey), I would reply with Buddhism as my 'faith', in a means to set me apart and feel obscure. Why then, did it still did not feel right? To those who were on the 'left side' on that fateful day in class. You may say that God let all these things happen. That otherwise, we would be in a heavenly utopia here on earth, where everything was perfect, and there were no problems in the world. As drastic as it may be for me to say this, I think we as humanity need these problems (within reason).

Now no one of any good nature wishes this on their worst enemy (or maybe do), but I think life itself without confrontation, would become very boring. Would we even consider it as being good as we would have nothing to compare it to? There would be no disasters, no challenges to learn from, and no reasons to reconcile. We are born with the potential to do both bad and good. Life is the chance to work out which potential we will live up (or down) to. That is the cycle that we must all go through as humanity. I have always taken great note to a particular line from the movie *Watchmen*, based on the graphic novel by Alan Moore. While being interviewed by a psychiatrist on the reasons for his vigilant ways, the protagonist Rorschach recounts the events that led up to the discovery of a young girl, who had been kidnapped, raped and murdered by a predator.

"See, doctor, God didn't kill that little girl. Fate didn't butcher her and destiny didn't feed her to those dogs. If God saw what any of us did that night, he didn't seem to mind. From then on, I knew: God doesn't make the world this way. We do".

As expressed by Orpah Winfrey, "God is a feeling experience and not a believing experience. If your religion is a believing experience...then that's not truly God". When we exclaim to ourselves "I will follow", it should not mean blindly trail without any ability to observe, think and reflect for yourself. It means, in my opinion, to be a bodily conduit for the force of light and love that, results in outward peace and compassion. I remember once on a film scholarship application I made a comment about creation making me feel like God. My mother immediately told me that it was blasphemous and egotistic to do so. I now understand what she meant.

With my search for improvement and self-understanding now in full ascension, I came across the philosophies of Lat Tsū, Confucius and Bruce Lee. To have a way of teaching that matched my own, was extremely relatable, so I was surprised when I found that these ways originated from a singular 'way' of teaching called Taoism (pronounced Dao). Unlike Buddhists who believe you must suffer here on earth to reach enlightenment; Taoist's believe that you can find happiness here on earth by following the Way of the Tao. This seemed 'it', the religion that I had been searching for. Why then, did I still feel that by identifying as Taoist, I wasn't truly serving my own spiritual consciousness? After much deliberation, and research into the history, culture and philosophy of theology as a whole, I came to the ultimate realisation that these are all the same.

The Path to God. Enlightenment. The Way. They all mean the same thing, just structured in a different way. Through historical, regional and cultural context. They all in one way or another, refer to this force (whether it be through a deity or spiritual path), The 'force' between us that, much like the Dream-time's connection to mother nature, surrounds us, binds us, and makes 'it' grow. Its energy (God/Tao) is where life here on earth springs from. Praying and meditating in essence are the same as well. Putting something that resides within yourself out into the ether. In my journey to self-realisation, I came to the conclusion that it is very much like creating a vibration force that is a reflection of your true-self. I always took solace in what George Carlin, the master of satirical comedy (ironically known for his distaste on religion as a human construct), referred to it as.

> "I think we are part of a greater wisdom, that we will ever understand. A higher order. Call it what you want. You know what I call it? The Big Electron. It doesn't punish, it doesn't judge at all, it just is. And so are we. For a little while".

Does God judge though? Does karma exist? Well, is there not a cause and effect for everything?

With this newfound outlook, I suddenly was able to look at these religions as is there was no name and pre-existing stereotypes attached to them. I saw them for what they had to say, as opposed to what they were and not seem them through the lens of judgement. I saw the teachings of Jesus Christ for example, with much greater clarity, separating the historical and cultural elements, while taking the spirit of what the message was. For those who seem doubtful in their faith, consider not only what you believe/feel, but why you believe it (a feeling), and most importantly, how far you believe/feel into it. Once I understood in principle, they all refer to the same things in essence, no longer was I separating myself by culture or dogmatic opinion. I was able to inquire, refer, and draw my own conclusions based on my own influence.

We become scared by the term religion and being religious. We think by being religious we have to be aligned under a great system of teachings. Now if that's what works for you, great, and while I the have utmost respect for the underlying messages, I believe you don't have to be deeply involved in their religious practices to feel a connection within yourself. What I feel is important however, is to take the essence of their principles, and work them into create understanding, meaning and peace to your own life.

I believe when I need to believe, whilst believing that we are no greater than the source of our existence, while knowing that our existence comes from within.

That, to me is the true definition of faith.

On the corner wall of my father's study, there is a painting. Transcribed from the poem by writer Max Ehrmann, it reads 'Found in Old Saint Peter's Church Baltimore. Dated 1692. (It is actually written by Ehrmann in 1927). I've known it was there for years, but never took that step to enquire about its message. Only then was I able to truly value its meaning.

DESIDERATA

Go placidly amid the noise and haste and remember what peace there may be in silence. As far as possible without surrender be on good terms with all persons. Speak your truth quietly and clearly: listen to others even the bull and ignorant: they too have their story. Avoid loud and aggressive persons, they are verations to the spirit. If you compare yourself with others, you may become vain and bitter: for there will always be greater and lesser persons than yourself. Enjoy your achievements as well as your plans. Keep interested in your own career, however humble, it is a real possession in the changing fortunes of time. Exercise caution in your business affairs; for the world is full of trickery. But let this not blind you to what virtue there is; many persons strive for high ideals; and everywhere life is full of heroism. Be yourself. Especially do not feign affection. Neither be cynical about love; for in the face of all aridity and disenchantment it is as perennial as the grass. Take kindly the things of youth. Nurture strength of spirit to shield you in sudden misfortune. But do not distress yourself with imaginings; many fears are born of fatigue and loneliness. Beyond a wholesome discipline, be gentle with yourself. You are a child of the universe; no less than the trees and the stars; you have a right to be here. And whether or not it is clear to you, no doubt the universe is unfolding as it should. Therefore, be at peace with God, whatever you conceive him to be, and whatever your labors and aspirations in the noisy confusion of life keep peace with your soul. With all its sham, drudgery and broken dreams, it is still a beautiful world. Be careful, strive to be happy.

Saying Things With Conviction
(Why Won't People Listen to Me?)

How often had you said something to someone, perhaps an idea or suggestion, only for to get ignored?

I can tell you from firsthand experience, this lack of conviction over others' attention was almost always the driving factor in creating feelings of doubt in myself. Even when deep down you know that the information or idea you have holds create value and promise, it is debilitating to find that no matter how hard you try, people still show no interest in your intention.

As discussed earlier, some individuals naturally have a commanding presence. Attributes that make people stop and listen. For you however, this may not be so easy. In most cases, those of small stature automatically have the challenge that even though you may stand out physically when compared to others, it becomes quite the opposite when trying to draw people's attention with your words. As your thoughts are reflected externally through your appearance (remember page 206), instead of commanding others through your presence, you have a much more subtle task of drawing them in through nonattachment. That means:

You don't care if they listen or not.

That may seem counter-productive and condescending, but as you have learnt throughout this journey; a man/woman who can detach themselves from the outcome is one who actually seems to have more things come their way. In most cases, as a result of being too concerned with other's approval, we draw on our emotions as a way of alleviating the disappointment. In this last-ditch effort, we hope those will understand and show some kind of sympathy towards us, but in doing so, we only push away these people we were trying to convince. You actually showcase yourself as someone who can't handle disappointment. By changing this one aspect of your response, we realise we actually don't have to respond. That time will come.

You may have heard the phrase; **Just believe in yourself**.

If you want your message to be received as intended, you first have to believe in the instrument that conveys that information. Think of it as not making someone listen, but rather as an opportunity to put yourself forward. If you want people to take note, first take note of yourself.

Referring back to Marshall McLuhan's quote on the 'medium being the message', it is behind what you say which dictates how it comes across. The medium, in this instance, is you. So, any worry, hesitation or nervousness about what others might think takes precedence. Apart of believing in yourself means to actually believe in what you are saying. Know your content inside and out to the point where no person or opposing information can contradict you (see page 256). Never <u>think</u> you know; telling people what they want to hear. Yes, it is natural for you to be nervous about all this, but this is only because you genuinely care and in reality, it is the right thing to do. If you know deep down this is the case, and it just takes waiting for the right time (as you will uncover later), and that step of doing, then you have no reason to have doubts.

It is an accumulation of all these principles you have learnt thus far; knowing that whatever it is you are saying, comes from a genuine place. Listen to what they have to say, and you will find by not attaching yourself, they will listen in return. If they don't, then perhaps another time.

How to Become Fluent at Public Speaking

Public speaking. I always loathed it at school. The dreaded idea of standing in front of and addressing people who couldn't care less about me. I vividly remember almost every-time I got up to begin my speech, the teacher would always have to quite everyone down as if they didn't even notice I were there. What followed was me timidly glancing up and down from my palm cards, no true relation or understanding of what I was saying or why.

Every-time, the critique from the teachers was the same. "Needs to look up. Talk louder. Clearer. Slower".

They would break apart how I did this wrong and needed to do this, but then did not follow up on teaching me actually how to. They only praised the other students who were naturally effortlessness and entertaining in their speeches. You may have seen countless others renowned for their skills in public speaking and crafting a performance. Actor's. Stand-up comedians. Self-help gurus. How could these people go up there and so confidently talk effortlessly without a care in the world?

When I was in prep-school, I could remember my speeches off by heart (most of the time). It was as if I was taking enjoyment in presenting. Going back to detaching from what others thought, this rapidly changed once I grew into adolescence and started obsessing about the evaluations and opinions of my 'peers'.

In conducting research aimed to regain that sense of power I once had in presenting, I came across a seminar by renowned entrepreneur and businessman, Dan Lok. Dan's story is one that is an example of the journey one takes in manifesting the true-self. Starting off as a Chinese immigrant who barely spoke a word of English, he later headlined as a head speaker of his own professional conferences. The following are my notes I expanded upon from that such presentation.

1. "All speaking is public speaking". Whether one on one or a large group, it is important to treat each conversation as that. A conversation. Natural and flowing. When we use the term 'public speaking', we immediately attach bad connotations that it is something different to talking. Don't see it as doing a speech with notes. See it as you sharing your experience and knowledge to others. The unselfish act of giving.

2. "Focus on the audience. Not yourself". They always say picture the audience naked, but I feel there is a better analogy. A much less traumatizing one. The audience is who you are trying to educate, so why would you see them as an issue? This is an opportunity to express yourself. Use them as a part of your performance. Relay off them. Remember true focus (chin and first and third levels). Look at their eyes.

I like to imagine that I am even not the one speaking, that behind me there is another person of higher importance, and I am just a part of the audience, turning around every so often to see the truth.

3. Power move. Have a gesture that immediately fires you up and calms all your fears. Being a student of martial arts (the philosophy of Jeet Kune do), Dan's move was to strike the air. For those not into martial arts, this can be breathing into your stomach to relax everything. Mine for example, is to extend my hand in a sarcastic, gesturing way. You can even use a mental image to put you in a good state of feeling. One that reflects what your true self is capable of receiving. Something that when you picture it, puts a smile on your face and changes your demeanour.

4. "Confidence comes from competence". In other words, practice! Remember when I said I could remember my speeches off by heart? Partly this was due to my impressive long-term memory, (this would later come useful in memorizing lines for drama performances) but also to the fact that I rehearsed.

Practice makes perfect. Apart of that practice is first believing in what you say, and secondly knowing and understanding your content to the point where you don't even have to think about it. Taking joy in sharing it to others.

5. Breathing and speaking. Refer back to the chapter on meditating and breathing. Speak from your diaphragm, NOT your chest. Test it out now. Speaking with conviction, means speaking with power. Your voice has twice as much depth when you talk from your stomach. It also allows you to speak more clearly. This is imperative in order for people needing to understand you. They can't take in your message if they can't hear it. Slow down, speak clearly. As you will learn later, it is much like being in time with the rhythm and beat of a song or dance.

6. Body language. This runs parallel to being interested in what you have to say as your body posture is a natural reaction of that. Shoulders back. Chest open. This does not mean in a selfish way (shoulders back exaggerated), but rather being able to create an open, inviting presence. Relaxed, but still focused. Focused, but present with your audience. Remember the circles of anxiety and control. As Lok expresses; **"Be interested, not interesting. When you say something, it means something, but when they say something, it means everything".** Your body language is the deciding factor that joins this dynamic together in harmonic totality.

How to 'Win' An Argument: A cure for all relationships

If you have looked down eagerly to find out the answer to this age-old question, I am sorry to say you have already failed. You cannot win an argument. Having been in the firing line, and sometimes the instigator of various arguments over the years, the need to win an argument is built on our ego and the need for being right. Whether it be between parents, friends or colleagues, they all result in the venting of your frustration, and standing firm of your beliefs. Does anyone really walk away the better off though? The real victim most often than not, is the irreversible damage it does to the already fragile human dynamic that are relationships. Friendships. Business partnerships. Marriages. Half of these fail because of the aftermath of heated arguments, which ultimately occur because of the unresolved issues within each individual.

"That's normal though", you say. "All couples go through it".

Disagreements are normal, yes. In that they represent the polar opposite of opinion and perspective in an issue. Yet, when these issues come to no conclusion, time and time again, year after year; this is a tell-tale sign that there is something deeper under the surface to resolve. The ability the get into a relationship is one thing, but the ability to hold it, continually, is another entirely. It shouldn't be something that we have to constantly keep walking on eggshells for, but something that just is. How many times have you heard this phrase?

'Women say men don't know how to communicate, and men say women are too emotional'.

Referring back to the dynamics of masculinity and femineity, half the time men fail so bad at communicating is because they have no idea how their lack of awareness towards their emotions effects their decision making and behaviour. They fear the scrutiny that comes with the idea of a man being vulnerable, whilst not knowing it is that lack of vulnerability that results in them not being understood. Ironically, on the other hand, the women are in agreement to the first half of the statement, only to erupt in a sea of anger at the sound of the second. It only proves the point. Stubbornness and denial are the two underlying reasons why couples of any kind can't evolve or solve their problems. If you disagree, what part of yourself are you defending? Stubborn to your own faults? Or denial of the truth that reveals such faults? Most often, we go into an argument with a **wall** set up to defend your internal good from outside forces. Do not confuse this with

boundaries. Unlike the former, the latter limits the expansion and effect on/of ideas and third parties.

"When you attach to an intention, you place a certain level of expectation around it and automatically limit yourself by creating parameters and boundaries around the potential outcome. Your manifestation is no longer in your highest interest but in your perceived idea of what your highest interest is."- Vernon Howard

Think back to when you first met your significant other. You were attracted to them for what they did with themselves in their own lives. Therefore, you must allow that space to exist once again. We need time for ourselves. Just as love is the space between you, you can easily suffocate that space with false habits that negatively impact your partner.

Note: It is easy to say we can just meet someone where this all isn't an issue? Perhaps. If that was the case, then would these concerns that were initially a problem, still exist towards other people? I feel if this was the case, then we wouldn't actually have learnt about ones-self, and the extent that our personality has across multiple scenarios. Going back to the equation, it is very much about the timing and crossing of paths that another goes down. The fixing of these faults, is often the prime reason for meeting our significant other. The need to control others often symbolizes the lack of control you have in yourself. You should never own your wife, husband, boyfriend, girlfriend or life partner. You should just simply be with them, enjoying each other's company and for who you both are as people. In the confides of a marriage, it is important to differentiate between what lens you see it through. A societal construct, legal contract, or existential pact between lovers.

Most say that their wedding day/honeymoon is the happiest moment in their lives. Yes, the lights, cake and dress may say so, but rather than attributing this feeling to a single moment in time, realise that the same feeling can exist every day. Even if you believe, after years of normal life taking hold, it is longer present. It is. It just is buried under our own pressures and priorities. Whenever we have an argument of any kind, it only pushes the dirt down even further. **Vulnerability is best used to evolve a relationship.** By that I mean through breaking the cycle of stubbornness in ones' self. Acknowledging your actions and accepting this state of denial. Only when one chooses to discard their overly-sensitive notions of self-pride (pride that isn't warranted/earned), can they develop passion for themselves, and subsequently, their partner.

Every time you look at your significant other, there is a moment for a split second where you understand why it is you love them. They are no longer a person with a name, a heart, a smile, lips and eyes, but they just are, the embodiment of a soul presented to you for your delight.

While writing this chapter, I was in deep discussion with a friend who days earlier had seemingly become frustrated with how I seemed so relaxed towards the situation; that I was hurting her. She was yelling and shouting and could feel her lack of awareness to her emotions was driving her behaviour. I thought of giving in and admitting I was wrong, but knew if I just kept calm, the authentic form of the conversation would reveal itself. Sure enough, she broke down, admitting that she had been going through some things, and that her outburst was just a way of her dealing with the overbearing guilt.

"I can't believe how sensitive I'm being right now".

"No", I replied. "You are just a gentle soul. A beautiful, gentle soul. Who's shy, but not shy philosophy gets you in trouble from time to time".

"I'm short tempered, but I've been working on that," she confessed. "I think that is what you need", I said. "To go through your own cycle, as part of that is a release. Women do it different to men. I close off. You open up. Me in sorrow. You in anger". I then told her the quote above. "Yes, it's so true".

Always be careful of the tone in which you tell something. By telling, there is the off chance that you can come across as demanding. Wanting a direct outcome, an outcome that is dependent on their understanding and cooperation. Think of it more as guiding through the direction of reality. The truth can hurt and will cause an impact, but rather it come through the warmth of a friend, then the icy sting of a stranger. Communicating means giving and receiving information, actually listening and genuinely being interested by what they have to say. It develops your understanding of the situation.

No-one, including yourself, wants to be proven wrong. It is not necessarily the words themselves, but the brash tone that does the damage. Remember the words of Marshall McLuhan. It is not what you say, but how you say it.

Rather than being angry or frustrated that you can't understand, be willing to want to understand. Likewise, rather than directing distaste towards your partner because they cannot understand your perspective, be willing to want to show them what it feels like from your end. LISTEN! We get so caught up in our own ego and need to be right that we lose to ability to pay attention.

A good tip that I discovered in the book, *Life's Little Instruction Book Vol II*, by H. Jackson Brown, Jr, reigns true. When in an argument, **"lower your voice to the amount that the other participant raised it".** You immediately make things a lot calmer, and show to your partner that you aren't here to belittle them or prove them wrong, but to seek to the common goal of understanding. This ultimately clears the space between the two people in question and relieves the tension. Tension only brought about by a lack of understanding and an influx of the ego (my opinion is right**). See it not as being someone you are talking to, but that you are talking to someone.** A full person, with fears, desires, a backstory as to why they are that way.

Through doing this, we are able to relate to their experience and struggles, and truly understanding why they are acting this way. Their emotion is justified. That is all it is. It is not necessarily them you are frustrated with, but the emotion that is a result. It is through gaining clarity on why this emotion is present, and relating it to your own plight, a common space occurs that is the bridge to deeper connection, and absolute resolution.

Becoming The Person, You Tried Not To Be
(Predicting Your Downfall)

You are at that stage in your transformation process now, where you have had multiple experiences driven by your true, higher self. The pure ecstasy you feel in this state is unrivalled. You relish in it, not for one second doubting whether you should let up. You have come so far from where you began, so the thought of going anywhere lower than is one you'll gladly forget. Then, out of nowhere, you are thrown a curve ball. One that shakes your newly found power and confidence, that is the sole reason that this chapter even exists in the first place. One that I am most grateful for.

I had just come from another day of work. Although fairly standard, with my newfound confidence, I was content and happy with myself being there. On the way to the cafeteria to retrieve my belongings, I saw my friend sitting outside the entrance. In the comfort of another friend (whom I knew), tears fell down her cheek. Immediately I went to inquire what was wrong. She looked up at me. Her eyes were filled with a sense of simultaneous sorrow and anger. Somehow, this involved me. The rest of the afternoon, thoughts ran rampant through my mind, making me question everything I had done. Everything I had achieved until now. I had this feeling of pride that I had been going about things the right way. Had I treated her wrongly? Had I treated others the same? In my own search for betterment, had I forgotten that part of me that was for the benefit of others?

You and Your Ego

This was the birth of a new defining moment, just from the other end of the spectrum. Most of the times we are not aware we are acting out of our ego. That is the double-edged nature of it. It masks our own awareness to our behaviour. "Wow, did I really sound like that? That was never my intention". This intention, no matter how its effect, is the crucial factor in recovering from the shock that self-realisation inflicts. In my experience, I was **subconsciously unaware** that this pre-occupied ego occasionally caused me to be somewhat narcissistic towards others whom I was trying to get to see a particular way in order to reach understanding for self-improvement. This wasn't me trying to please others, but was more attempting to please myself through creating a genuine dynamic. To generate reciprocation. What I did not realise is their understanding was based on something I cannot create, force, and control. They had to do for themselves, just as I had to 'earn it', by earning myself. I had to let them go their own way. Now on the opposing side, there are those who are **consciously aware** of their ego, and take delight in looking down on others. We know this is due to an unresolved part of themselves at play, and even though it can cause deep embarrassment to address this, it is more valuable to apologise for one's actions, then it is to affirm your false-self. Going back to genuine intention, ask yourself deep down what your intention was and more importantly why? Was it out of fear? Jealousy? Regret? Anger? We think by resisting, we are being strong, but by doing so, we only supress our dormant emotions. Don't believe me? Bring your hands up and squeeze hard. Now hold it. That same tension you are experiencing is resisting in its simplest form. (See page 134).

How To Come Down from A High Ego?

After much reflection, my initial response was to do nothing. Just take some time, and let it pass. This only caused my friend to fight back, demanding why I was being so distant? In my quest to put myself first, I had subsequently failed to treat my friend in a way that acknowledged her ability and lessened her potential. Yes, that was because that was all I could go off, but this insightful moment showed me a side to her that I needed to witness. A side that made me experience humility.

When you come across crossroads such as these, a good analogy that I have taught myself is that you have to misunderstand one another's perspective in order to get to the perspective that is higher than all. At this very moment you are going through the moment that they too will go through. Consider the other's perspective. Try to see where they are coming from. A place other than yourself. It's not that your viewpoint isn't right, but rather how much value does it hold in proper existence? (Structured perspective).

Which Is Easier?

You might be curious to ask whether from which position is it easier to transform from? From the initial observation, it would seem that it is harder for the cocky one to change, as everything has worked for them, and therefore has no reason to. However, on the opposite end, the person who has been subjected to unfairness and created feelings of distaste towards him/herself, has all the reason in the world to change. To me, they are both equally one of the same, whilst being different. Only until an event happens that shifts their outlook on things, will they start the questioning necessary to change. The constant that is also its defining factor. The individual.

The individual could be the one newly in touch with their true self, that confronts the cocky one in a way that causes them to experience humility.

Or

The individual could be the uncompassionate one that has trod down on the other, to a point where it causes them to start a journey of self-confidence.

In this cycle, understanding bridges all things together harmoniously. Without conflict, there can be no opportunity for understanding. With understanding, conflict ceases to exist. Regarding the insightful moment I experienced above, the guilt that I would have initially experienced was lessened to the fact that I remembered it wasn't just about understanding their perspective, but indirectly, my own.

When You Reach The Limit

Throughout this book we have stressed the point to constantly be evolving. That in order to achieve success, you must keep building momentum, with anything that cannot be sustained past the surface level as to having no value. However, as I'm sure you have become aware of, there comes a point in the transformational journey where you have depleted every avenue you can out of a particular scenario or environment. That, no matter how hard you try to continue on the path that is your true self, you find yourself back making mistakes, creating doubt. This is a sign that you have reached the limit. The first step in combating this, is to understand this cycle is normal, and present in all forms of nature. From the seasons where things are nurtured, bloom, then welter away, to the lunar phases of the moon, your own transformation process goes through the exact same sequence. The climb, the peak, then the fall. What follows after, is you coming to the crossroads of two choices:

A) Keep being sad. Do you want things to stay this way?

B) Have courage and do something about it.

The bridge between these two choices (from a to b), is where a problem arises. As we cannot identify what state we are actually in, we are never able to traverse over into the next stage of moving on, and thus either stay or fall further into the damaging proponents that encourage our false-self. After going through the events that brought my ego back down to earth, I realised that there was a pattern. Upon reflection, I summarised each of these states in a sequence.

The Cycle of Transformation

State of Depression
State of Selfishness
State of Being
State of Ego
State of Humility
State of Unselfishness

State of Depression
State of Selfishness
State of Being
State of Ego
State of Humility
State of Unselfishness

Just as outlined in the chapter on momentum, by observing the cycle that your emotional state follows, you can easily move up and down 'the scale' with ease. Once I could identify the various stages of my transformation I was going through, I was able to know what things I needed to do to seamlessly move onto the next.

State of Depression: We start at a place where our outlook towards ourselves and our life is dire. The bottom of the rabbit hole. In order to even begin to pull ourselves out, we have to start to focus purely on ourselves.

State of Selfishness: Simply. Bring things back to you. This at first may come across as selfish, but if you reassure yourself, this is the right thing to do for you, then all your doubt goes away.

State of Being: This is where you taste your first glimpse of togetherness and totality. Everything comes naturally to you, and you discover a sense of wonder and excitement in things that you never felt before. You also reveal this additional level of confidence, motivation and momentum.

State of Ego: You feel this great level of sureness within yourself; however, it is now backfiring. Caught up in your own newfound success, you slowly turn your back on those around you and in turn, take your situation for granted.

State of Humility: Your ego has reached its point of no return. Those who once held you in high regard are now retaliating in anger at your lack of empathy and understanding. In this sudden state of unpreparedness, you encounter a feeling and you haven't experienced in a long time. Humility.

State of Unselfishness: Now begins the embarrassing task of trying to prove your forgiveness and show your empathy. This means dropping everything that you are doing and solely working for the betterment for others.

State of Depression: You once again have become a doormat to your false-self. In fear of hurting others for a second time, you will do everything anything to please others for your sense of pride. Sadly, in doing so they lose all control over the say in their life and their being, and the cycle starts again.

Note: We confuse the state of being and unselfishness as being one of the same. We associate unselfishness as a fundamental part of our true self and therefore do everything to please everyone.

As we know, depending on our perspective, there is a difference between **unselfish selfishness, and selfish unselfishness.**

You can't chaperon people all the time, even if it is based on good intentions. You need to let them be independent, make their own mistakes, then guide once they return.

Referring back to the process of self-learning, most often than not we can become stuck in a cycle of repetitive failures. Infuriated when we make a mistake, we expel all our energy in hopes to rectify it. Unaware to us, it, like our emotional state, this only rises, culminating to defeatism. What is the solution? Well, just like thoughts, failure (and mistakes) comes and go. Move on. Let things settle. Things, once they rise, will fall. The success you are capable of will come back into the sequence of the cycle.

Towards the beginning of this book, I referred to Muhammad Ali and his thoughts that boxing was a tool of expression for himself. In another interview with Dick Cavett, when discussing his second career loss to Leon Spinks, he said the following.

> *"I've been on top so long it's good to fall sometimes and realise where I was, so I can come back and appreciate it, so sometimes I don't mind getting beat".*

He later won back the title in a rematch.

On a much smaller scale, I could now identify all the various intricacies of the cycles in my life. From career paths to relationships, arousal and emotional levels. Even attempts at transforming my body. It was now clear that whenever I started again, I would implement the following.

Call this a condensed summary.
- Cleaning up room and table
- Forming a morning routine (making bed, stretching, etc)
- Setting aside time for a project
- Starting a form of active mediation or fitness regiment
- Abolishing any form of vice, poor habit or addiction

We view this higher state as something that we need to strive for. That no other state will suffice. We become attached to returning to the feelings we once relished in, and so begins the desperate search for the return. There is no need to search. All that you require is already there. In my own quest to transform my being from the 'nice guy' into something more confident, I realised even though I had made changes and progressed thusly, in the grand scheme of things, I had not changed at all. I had come full circle to the conclusion that I was still the same person, just refined. I was still a nice guy, but now instead of it being founded from insecurity, it was coming from sureness in self. Remember that lecturer who once provided me insight into my premature way of thinking? He also told me I have to use what we determine as our weakness to our advantage. Develop it in such a way that, in a certain context, it is no longer a weakness, but a superpower. Put everyone you may have concerns with aside, and bring everything back to you. Relay that foundation. Pinpoint what this anxiety is directed towards, and distance yourself from all things associated with that, then slowly without trying, you will find yourself back at that state. It will be as if you never left.

Everything Is Everything

Despite coming to terms with the cycles that ran alongside my own introspection, I still had this lingering concern that I could not seem to shake. That, despite their clearly being this higher truth or 'way' to things, people still see things a certain way, and others, another.

In attempting to understand every single avenue and component of an issue, I became deeply confronted with the task of justifying why it is these exist, even though they shouldn't. It got to the extremes where, it was almost excruciatingly troublesome to comprehend. Putting aside my own opinions, I explicitly imagined myself in their shoes. From their own angle, albeit extremely construed, I could see how they could see it that way. There was, however miniscule, some form of truth to them. Ironically though, as soon as I introduced another component or perspective to question its validity, this truth crumbled into obscurity. Like a stone being thrown into a pond, the ripples created dissipate on top of one another, settling until there is nothing left but what was before the impact. Thus, this led me to forming a mantra of my own creation. An ultimate philosophy that upholds the universal laws of all the chapters that have come before.

> Everything means everything, whilst
> meaning nothing simultaneously

Everything that can exist, does. Instead of trying to justify its reasons for existing, or why it shouldn't, realise there is a better way. It may have formed together, but at what cost? Referring again to boundaries and limits, once you go past a certain point, you lose the distinct meaning it was founded upon, taking it to a meaning it (while able to exist), has no depth. Meaning without meaning to. As highlighted in the path of least resistance; too many barriers and the flow of naturalness becomes blocked. In this instance, sometimes it is required for things to stay in their separate lanes, to act as layers or levels. When there are no obstructions, anything can pass through, and it is difficult for people to distinguish the truth. In their collective minds, it is their own personal truth. An incomplete one. Perhaps I am too concerned with forming the truth in/for others you say. That I should be more focused on myself. Look into a person's eyes. Stare at them long enough, and your vision will pass through all the projected illusion they hide behind, until you see the only thing that remains. Their universe. (See page 233). Your truth may be different to others, but it ultimately revolves around the same principles. They are just brought about at different times, by diverse aligning circumstances. See it like this. There is a vase which sits atop a small table in the centre of your living room. If you were to stare at it, but through the guise of a window, the extent to which you could comment its features would be dependent on;

- Where it is you are standing. The angle, distance and height.
- The amount of light which shines through the window.
- Whether you are inside looking in, or inside looking out.

We have found the absolute truth, when there is nothing that can possibly contradict its own existence. We have found the higher perspective, when, after all that has been acted upon (cause), there is nothing that can be held accountable to its direct consequence (effect). Just like a piece of artwork, life can be subjective. That is perhaps both its greatest success, and irreversible failure.

How to Read the Situation & Act Accordingly
i.e., Overthinking Revisited

How often have you gone into a situation feeling as it will go one way, only for the opposite to happen? "How could I have read that so wrong"? We desperately try so hard to read a situation, wonder what action to take, and in doing so get all flustered when it does not turn out as we hoped. In struggling to desperately return to this higher state we are forgetting one thing. Our experience as a conscious individual resolves around the connection between the parameters of a subconscious entity entirely unto itself. A situation.

Being In the Moment

We say 'be in the moment', but what does this actually mean in relation to our own ability to hold a conscious experience? That is the key word; experience. Not only must we be able to read a situation, but subsequently, experience it for its true nature. Free from all falsities.

Recall back to a memory in your life where you know you were in flow. When you picture this feeling of the experience, you immediately will find yourself in a state of flow that resembles your own. One that reflects what your true-self can receive. Remember the words by Iyanla Vanzant; Not the feeling, not the excitement, but the experience. From personal experience, this works best when you abolish expectation from everything you go into. Don't assume. Even when assuming not to.

Clear all thought from your mind. Disassociate yourself with all forms of media that hold one-dimensional messages to be misconstrued or misinterpreted later. It is interesting to observe how easily it was to exist purely in the moment, once you don't have all these influences confusing your subconscious. Ultimately, all they do is act as blockades to letting the experience come through. The next time you become uneased by a potentially unsettling incident, go through the following;

1. Open your awareness to the context (surroundings) in which you are in.
2. Read the intention 'aura' of others associated within that context.
3. Know your own intention (sometimes to may be to have none). And more importantly, how to counteract it.
4. Listen to your intuition (emotional content) that lies within. **If something doesn't feel right, think. If you have to think about something, what does your gut feeling tell you?**
5. If it is too much. Do nothing. Let the proper beat in the sequence come back into alignment.

Trusting In Your Ability: Timing Is Everything

Now having read back on this book, hopefully you will have gained an insight into how your internal and external factors affect one another, and more importantly, practical ways to implement this knowledge. Whether it be a confronting event or argument, by trusting our ability to see these things as they are, and the limits that come with each, we will automatically be better equipped to address any doubt that may cross our minds. By having this ability to adapt to your surroundings, you are able to react to any situation appropriately. It is here where our mind and body are one. Completely synchronized.

Remember back to the chapter on 'being the better man'. Some situations require solely to practice direct timing, patience, or to follow a certain rhythm. Most often, it is a combination of all these bouncing back and forth with one another, where you are free from reacting from outside emotion, and acting through inner contentment. Technique with no technique. You are a part of the orchestra composition that creates the melody. The dancer following the beats of the song. Work with the timing, not against it. Experience it as intended, in the right context, the right amount, and the appropriate time in the sequence (refer back to page 69). Again, it is very much an equation, only this time, the underlying factor is the context in which both parties are restrained, or in some cases freed by. When we constantly have these one-dimensional thoughts at the forefront, it only distorts and delays the underlying truth and moment that we deeply desire. Peel back the layers to your consciousness, and your conscious will guide you forth with the better way. That is the true power of introspection.

You + other + <u>context</u> = outcome

Another way to comprehend this, is through the glass half-full/empty analogy. In terms of overthinking, your potential to be truly harmonious with a moment, free from the subconscious extremities of expectation, is dependent on;
- The current level the water is at. (Your mental state).
- The width and depth of the glass. (Context of moment).

- How quickly you fill it with thought, and how this competes with the space of the environment. (Approach).
- Negative thought can either drain the water, with optimism filling it, or can fill it on its own to the point it overflows.

There are so many quotes surrounding the whole analogy of half-full empty glass. These perspectives, although seemingly different, are ultimately irrelevant. By having controlled thoughts (or none at all), you can fill/drain the 'cup' when necessary. Small increments, or large. When its overflows in a negative way, empty it.

> "It does not matter if the glass is half-empty or half-full. All that matters is that you are the one pouring the water"- Mark Cuban

> "Some people see the glass half full. Others see it half empty. I see a glass that's twice as big as it needs to be". George Carlin

There is no glass. No water. You should be able to hold any substance that comes your way. Sometimes, the situation may require more than a glass. Sometimes there may be more than water that flows in. So, if you constantly feel like you can't catch a break. Try letting it come to you.

Like a surfer waiting for the perfect wave;

They sit. They wait. Swaying beneath a sea of raging emotion anchored to the shoreline of their mind. They watch. They listen. Expelling all worry or anxiousness, so that it washes out with the tide and out into the evermore. They know without knowing. Ready, but not expecting. Communicating through complete calm and limitless fluid motion. Until they let go. In a surge of what was, for a split moment, the foaming of rapids and parting of the deep,

was now was a graceful dance across water. They and the wave are one, a mix of monotone water colours and spiritual cacophony. They and the moment are now together
As if they were never apart.

Remember the point on accepting addiction and time being irrelevant? On closer inspection, I believe this state of flow we aspire to achieve turns more into a continuous state of momentum. Not straying from the line or path one has set themselves on. Each thought has its own effect. To find a state of being, we must balance it out with another. Sometimes, that 'other' is no thought at all.

Where to Go From Here?

On September 6th, 2010, I found myself sitting in an amphitheatre amongst one hundred other high school students. Our attention (for the most part) was fixed on a man that stood centre stage. Tall and stoic, he at first kept silent in his demeanour, but once he spoke, his words were soft, yet commanding. That man's name was Glen Gerreyn, the motivational speaker and accomplished author of *Get Your Hopes Up* and *Men of Honour*. He each handed us a copy of a small blue and white booklet, with the title; DAY of HOPE: EDUCATION, EXCELLENCE, EMPOWERMENT. On the first page, there were these three fundamental questions that he openly invited you to ask yourself.

1. Who am I?
2. Why am I here?
3. Where am I going?

I remember watching my fellow student observing how they took in this surge of information. Some were less than convinced, while others, despite relating to what he was saying, I knew as soon as they left, would forget it instantly. Myself on the other hand, felt a surge of energy, so much so that I began to answer these very questions questioning everything that was happening to me. It was the early (albeit premature) beginnings of my quiet, 'nice guy' shell breaking.

I rediscovered this very booklet one day while organising my cabinets full of old papers and works of a forgotten past. Although I never thought this would become such an important chapter in this manuscript, below are some of the more poignant notes Glen had us write. Much like the philosophy of self-learning and cycle of transformation.

1. Take the seed and plant it with good soil.
2. Nurture and water it. (Work on your talent).
3. Pull out weeds. (Negativity, habits, vices).
4. Goes through seasons. (Highs & lows/success & failure).

Glen said the reason to his success was passion **not** skill. Yes, you must acquire skills, but if those skills don't have a driving force behind them, they are just things you know. Passion will give you clues to your purpose, and *"nothing satisfies the human spirit more than purpose"*.

The two most important days in your life.
1. The day you were born. You came with a purpose.
2. The day you discover why. That purpose!

"It is meaninglessness that is society's greatest threat".

"If you don't get to the problems, then you won't get solutions".

"If you don't stand for something, then you will fall or anything".

I could have very well opened the book with this defining moment in the amphitheatre, including all these questions, sayings and mantras. However, in order to start a new foundation, it is crucial to tear down the old one first. Now that your house is ready to be built, you can use these questions to construct the structure. There is no point answering these questions, then after going through the process, coming back to them again. You need to ask new questions, to ensure you are able to excel forward. Therefore, I ask these three questions of you.

1. When do you know things are working?
2. When do you know things are not working?
3. What things do you do to go in and out of these?

I'd hope by reading through this book, you will have become truly aware of your traits, fears, desires and habits to be able to answer these. By knowing where it is you have come from, and knowing where you sit now, you can begin the journey of accumulating what it is you need to get there. Take a piece of paper and write down what it is you now know about yourself. Take as much time as you need, only writing down when true inspiration and focus comes through. By having the honesty towards what works for you, what doesn't and how you react as opposed to act, you have pieced together the final part of the door that you will soon walk through. This book has done its job as the springboard to your transformation experience. Now go out and finish it by creating your own.

In his Book, *The Tao of Jeet Kune Do,* Bruce Lee concluded that; **"When there is no centre and no circumference, then there is truth".** At first, I could not fathom what this exactly meant, only noting that it could mean inside-out or outside-in. I drew comparison for 'no circumference' to true focus, the circle of anxiety and control. Then, as my understanding of myself grew, and the development of my own concepts in the later end of this chapter, I realised it is so much more. Referring to the cycles and process of self-learning, it is breaking things up and down, inside and out. In relation to your headspace, you must trust in your intuition. To let everything form together and work. To be accepting and patient in letting things come your way. By having no boundaries through circumference and centre, there is no limitation. The truth can pass through without resistance because there is no truth. It just is.

"A very important moment in the work on oneself is when a man begins to distinguish between his personality and essence".
George Gurdjieff

There is one more question I implore you to ask yourself. One that will resolve any doubt and periods of stagnation.

Am I still pursuing?

If so, good keep going. If not, regardless how bad it may seem. Pick yourself up and start again.

Disclaimer: Is This Book Ultimately Pointless?

As there is a natural opposite to all things, inherently I know that, for whatever reason, this overall philosophical message that I am promoting would be susceptible to criticism. The idea that self-help books are pointless if the motivation to acquire one is already there, extends to the overall notion that philosophy provides no real value in society. The closer I became to completing this manuscript, the more I came across single pieces of spiritual information. From little mantras and words of wisdom that summarised the overall message of various sections I had written, to the Hermetic Principles outlined in the *Kybalion: A study of the Hermetic Philosophy of Ancient Egypt and Greece*; it seemed as if all the effort and analysis I had done was utterly irrelevant. Why go to this trouble writing a book when they could have easily been given these lessons to live by? Is all this work that you have done on one's self ultimately for no need?

Over the years of accumulating knowledge from a variety of diverse sources, I came across yet another interview from the Dick Cavett show. This time with the prolific film actor, writer and director, Orson Welles. Throughout the course of the interview, they came upon the topic of his education, with Welles exclaiming in desperation not to be educated, he rejected a scholarship to Harvard and went into the theatre. "I made it. I wasn't educated". The conversation then turned in Cavett asking Welles what he would have studied if the desire to study arose. "Everything, I guess. But if I wanted to study seriously, and get good at a subject, I think it would be anthropology. Don't you think that is a fascinating subject?" Cavett then suggested maybe philosophy, ironically remarking he "never really thought about it that much". Welles then said the following;

> "I'm suspicious of philosophy. I have a real philistine doubt about its worth, you know? But anthropology seems to me just at its beginnings, and philosophy, kind of at its end".

Even after much deliberation with myself, I couldn't understand what he possibly meant. Was it perhaps the fact, over the thousands of years philosophy has existed, it has indeed failed (given history's events and today's current landscape)? Is more of an anthroponomic outlook required to understand human behaviour as a whole? Not to sound any more magmatic than I have, but yes and no. For one, you could read all these sayings, and find a great amount of resonance and solace through their message, but have no in-depth knowledge of how this relates to yourself, and then further, how to implement them in accordance to your current stage of life. This is, and I agree, I major criticism of philosophy (and perhaps what Welles was referring to). In that it has become an imitation of itself, transformed into the limiting materialistic form of flowery phrases; something that is reserved for only the pretentious, highly cultured intellectual, or the airy-fairy spiritual. You become so enthralled through the liberation you feel from this new outlook, that you become overly accepting about everything and everyone.

This makes a strong point for anthropology, that an in-depth study of one's behaviours are the only way of unearthing transformative results. To this I would absolutely agree, as realistically speaking, we need this structure to provide real-time feedback to the individual.

However, as you progress further, you may discover the following. You have done all this work on knowing yourself, the origins of your anthropomorphic nature and idiosyncrasies, to come to the realisation that, in a grandiose natural way, things are as they are meant to be. Like an equation, whichever path you may take, any event that may have occurred were there to put to on a path to be resolved.

This is also true, however, from a purely pragmatic standpoint, what are these events determined by? The nature of human beings. I feel young people are in such a hurry to accomplish things. To grow up and receive success so quickly. They are influenced by the belief that they need to be perfect from the day they are born. They may achieve this success, but in doing so, how much knowledge about themselves have they learnt? Can they then teach this to those outside their normal realm? When the success that they so sought-after wanes (and it will), what lessons would they be able to take away? How much of themselves would they be left with? You need the dark days to challenge, to grow. It is in these moments that you understand perfection, while existing, is made up of smaller imperfections, that without, wouldn't be able to reveal the light that exists beyond.

What does this mean? To put it justly; It is alright to be imperfect sometimes, as in its particular moment, is most perfect. Perfect in that it redirects you to the next step in your journey to enlightenment. Imperfection exists to show there is a better way. Is philosophy as a whole, pointless? Is this entire book, and the pursuit of one's solace for no reward? That is for you to question, explore, experience, and then decide.

This Only Happens In The Movies

At the beginning of this book, you were presented with the scenario of you waiting behind a curtain, and the proceeding dream-like events that followed. This may seem like a fantasy, but this was indeed a glimpse into your true higher-self in action and the seemingly effortless way things would happen. I described a person who was calm, confident and able to communicate effortlessly without hesitation. It was almost as if it was something that could only happen in the movies.

"But those things never happen in real life", you say. "It only happens to movie stars or perfectly written characters". Well, yes, on the surface level is true, but ask yourself, what do all these people have in common? They are cool, collected and are fully present in the moment. "Wait a moment", you say. "How can something that is so scripted like a movie's events seem so natural?".

A person whose career and story I deeply relate to and follow is film maker and critic, Chris Stuckmann. In a review discussing the correlation between unnatural events and forced dialogue, he said the following.

> *"The magic of film is that you watched events that are controlled and planned, yet they feel spontaneous if the film is good."*

Although this may seem like fantasy, and indeed it is, it is crucial to distinguish this from reality. Again, ask what has to be in existence in order for it to occur? From this we can take a great deal, notably understanding how a person at a higher state can react. It's not what happens to you, but how you react to it that matters.

Reactive Action or Active Reaction

I returned finally to Vernon Howard's book and the red cover that started it all. On the right-hand side, below the title, I noticed the indentation of a series of shapes of what resembled rays of sunshine emerging from an inner circle. Looking deeper, underneath the surface level of what I thought they originally were, I interpreted this image as representing a teaching much more central to what he was transcribing. This, along with the symbol of Bruce Lee's own Jeet Kune Do Philosophy, inspired me to create my own. It was a decision that felt natural. Not something based on purely being like those before, but a proverbial force of genuine intention, that communicated to me; this feels right.

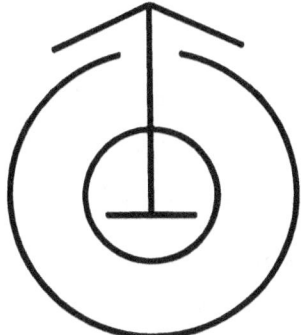

This symbol represents these core elements.

The Outer Circle: The circle of anxiety. Everything outside this causes you no problem. No fear. The cycle of perception.

The Vertical Line: The cycle breaks with you. This acts like the structure, working its way down to the closed sanctum of our essence. The third side to the coin.

The Inner Circle. The circle of control. Everything in here is under your responsibility. Likewise, everything that comes out into the outer circle is of your consequence.

The Horizontal Line: The foundation of utmost importance. Balance. Become unstable at any stage, and the structure and the scales fall.

The Peak: The roof of the structure. The goal. The higher perspective of enlightenment we all try to strive towards. Yet we don't realise it is already there and always has been. It is the symbolic illustration that we create everything that we do, yet we are no higher than what has created us. Once we have reached here. It is as if we are looking down on things. As if we see them through heaven's eyes.

After some observation, I chose to extend this concept further, introducing branching awareness and the lines bringing it onto our centre. The horizontal line still symbolizing balance, but now rooted at the base of the foundations.

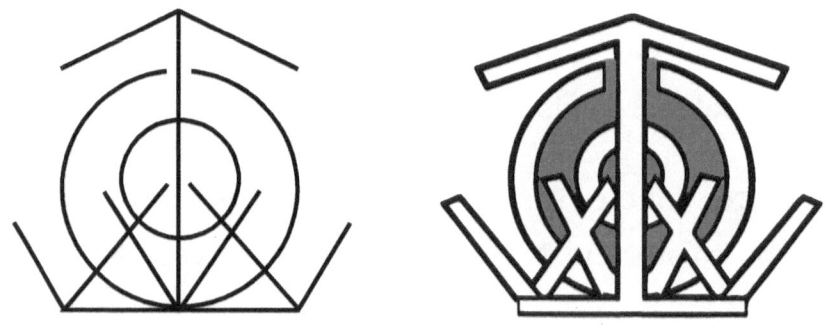

Although this may have seemed complete in terms of absolution, I felt there was still more to be discovered. Soon enough, I came across an image of a bridge situated in Kromlau, Germany. Known as the Rakotzbrücke, or Devil's Bridge, I found the sight of the arched structure reflected in the crystal-clear water captivating. It was this image alone that brought me back to my own personal mantra.

> **Everything means everything,**
> **whilst meaning nothing simultaneously**

This combined with, the reflection of the bridge, allowed me to draw comparisons, and thus extend the image of my creation further.

Now, I could have ended it there, but my inner voice was speaking to me, demanding I take it to its highest potential.

It was around this time I was taking note of the inherent cycles that were occurring both in my life and the wider world. It became almost like a common denominator. What rises, must fall. What goes up, comes down. Just like the process of learning. Breaking things down to its simplest form, then building them back up again. It was this distinct philosophy that allowed the symbol to take its final step.

Leaving My Island

Printed on the desk where I wrote the majority of this book, is a large overhead map of the *Cosmopolitan world: On Mercator's Projection*, by Rand McNally. When I asked the question, how big is your world? I found it fitting that although immensely insignificant by comparison, our own plight (in our own minds), is just as tumultuous if not more perilous than if we were to navigate the globe.

My mother once told me that "**life is not about discovering yourself. It is about creating it**". Taking what you have now and building it up to where it all works together. Through creating you will discover, and through discovery you will create a higher awareness to you and your surroundings. She has always been that one person who, despite sharing a similar struggle in her own personality to mine, believed in my capabilities. Others who thought that my prematurity did not impact me currently in life, would be remined by her that it did, but that was in itself, my greatest achievement. That I am still here, as an example the potential one has if they keep fighting. If they never give up. I know that through me sharing this book, she too will the regain essence of pure strength, love and resolve that brought me into the world.

In the final year of college, I wrote a series of poems as part of a portfolio. Entitled; *Leaving my Island*, never could I have known it would hold such relevance here. I feel this one best encapsulates the symbolic casting off my true-self into the horizon.

> *Shadowed by an over-arching banana leaf,*
> *a constant reminder of my failures,*
> *I sit on a lonely island,*
> *a castaway of broken dreams.*
> *Success seven lucky seas away.*
> *Treading knots upward to the surface*
> *of the forlorn existence anchored to my heels.*
> *I'm now talking to a coconut. Hungry for a vessel that may never come.*

But say that boat comes, from the depths of opportunity. By God, I'll swim to it.
The sails igniting an ember towards a horizon from which,
I'm viewing someone else eighty years from now on a distant island. Wondering.
Where they went wrong.

This book was, like any virtuous voyage, was a phenomenal process of reflection, repetition and realisation. By that I mean it was, in itself, a cycle. I thought it would be fitting to close this whole journey by bringing you back to where things all began. Ironically, things have come full circle. You realise it has been there all along. No longer are you tangled up in your web of disillusion. The tomb has opened itself from the inside, and only now are you ready to see the value it holds. One day, you may come across those who have done wrong by you in the past. When this day comes, they may see this new state you are in a exclaim, "You have changed!" Reply, "No. It is not me that has changed, but **your perception of me** that has. Only it is through your initial perception of me, that I looked inside to change the perception of myself. It that is why you see this 'change' before you". I once asked you to imagine a vision of your true-self in action. Now, take that same person, and distance yourself from it. As if you are viewing it from the audience or on a screen. With no knowledge or relation to their likeness, see them as an entirely different entity altogether. What initial perceptions about 'them', would come to mind? Will they like what they see? Will they then want to change?

On the precipice of the end, I felt that a final piece of clarity was needed before I could close off this manuscript for good. Not surprisingly, it once again encompassed the abundant bearings of thought, and in particular, the section on achieving true focus. During one particular session of active meditation, I was struggling to naturally calm my mind and be at completely one with my task. I found I was in a cycle of perception of my own. As soon as we recognise that we are disjointed in ourselves, and know there is this higher level we must strive to, we frantically shift through our thoughts to ones that take us forward. Yet, in being aware we are trying to dissolve them from our mind (to simultaneously evolve us) we only prolong their stay. How then? How does one return to this state of attention, without actively knowing you are trying to do so?

What is to dissolve? Take that word away. What is attention? Perhaps not to have any. What is thought? Take that away. What is mind? It is all non-existent. Take that word away too. What is all this in relation to me? There I realised. Me exists. To 'forget' the 'form' that is 'me' entirely. It was then that, for the 'first time' in a 'while', 'I' sat outside 'myself' at total 'peace'. Just as life began at nothing, so does it end with such. In complete silence.

As we get older, we find life keeps getting exponentially faster, while we are becoming slower and slower. Why is it, despite wishing it was the other way round, we fight it? Rushing ourselves for no apparent reason. Depending on whether the object is moving, you will either have to go one of two ways to successfully unite body with mind. Forward, or back. Advance to meet, or distance to give space between you and the object. The key to all of this, is that your head position stays put. Central. Fixed to the moment.

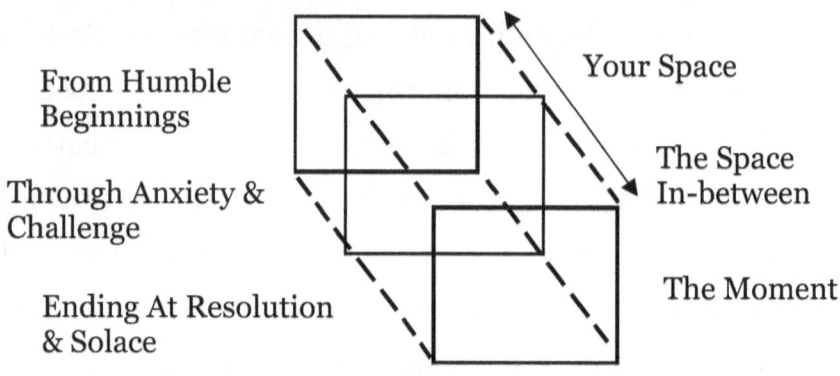

Note: Adhere to the levels of true focus and circles of anxiety and control. These squares or 'spaces' can shift back and forth depending on your state of being. The 'goal' (despite there being to have none), is to seize an opportune moment, to express your yourself, and by yourself, I mean your true essence.

In regards to the quickening of our journey, always take that split second longer, to sit within the moment. Slow down on purpose. See how long that wave will then carry you. Only speeding up, when necessary. To the point where everything gets left behind in your wake of momentum. Remember, there is no deadline to life, as is there none to our personal transformation.

Take solace in knowing that no matter which side we run along the river bank, the current always is directing us to a destination. Only once we have enough knowledge and trust in our abilities, will we be able to cross the bridge that presents itself when the time is right. Until then, anything else is neither here nor there.

With that, I leave you with a phrase I once wrote on a birthday card to my brother. Although it came from the ether, I believe it resembles a principle that is timeless.

If living is a part of life, then life should be worth living.

Works Referenced/Bibliography

Books

Deida, D. (2008). *The Way of the Superior Man*. Read How You Want Ltd.

Dyer, W., 1993. *You'll See It When You Believe It: The Way To Your Personal Transformation*. 1st ed. Vauxhall, London: Random House.

Ely, H., 2003. *The International Library of Poetry: THE COLOURS OF LIFE*. Watermark Press.

Howard, V., 1966. *Psycho-Pictography: The New Way to Use the Miracle Power of Your Mind*. 4th ed. West Nyack, New York: Parker Publishing Company.

MacLaine, S., 1989. *Going Within: A Guide for Inner Transformation*. 1st ed. United States & Canada: Bantam Books.

Merton, T., 2005.No Man Is an Island, Boston, Shambhala.

Millman, D., 2000. *Way of the Peaceful Warrior*. California, US: H.J. Kramer.

Jr, Brown, Jackson, H.,1993. *Life's Little Instruction Book Vol II: A few more suggestions, observations, and reminders on how to live a happy and rewarding life*, Melbourne, Australia, Bookman Press.

Lee, B., 1975/2018, *Tao of Jeet Kune Do: Expanded Edition, 14th Edition*, USA, Black Belt Books.

Interviews/Presentations

Ali, M., 1978. *The Dick Cavett Show*.

Friedman, M., 1980. *Free to Choose: I, Pencil*,

Lok, D., 2016. *Mental Tricks to reduce your fear of public speaking.*

Sowell, T., 2005. *Fox News Special: In the Right Direction.*

Stuckmann, C., 2015. Star Wars Episode III: Revenge of the Sith.

Van Dyke, D., 1974. *The Dick Cavett Show.*

Welles, O., 1970. *The Dick Cavett Show.*

Perry, M. and Hitchens, P., 2013. *BBC Newsnight.*

Films

The Secret of My Success. 1987. [film] Directed by H. Ross, A. Carothers, J. Cash and J. Epps, Jr [Screenplay]. Universal Pictures.

Watchmen. 2009. [film] Directed by Z. Snyder. Warner Bros. Pictures, Paramount Pictures.

Articles/Excerpts

Blackman, K., 2018. Great sex involves exquisite pacing. [Blog] *The interplay between pleasure and desire explained*, Available at: <https://medium.com/straight-talkers/when-to-speed-up-or-slow-down-and-how-to-tell-76262a8d5af6> kenblackmann.com.

Ehrmann, Max, Copyright Claimant, and Bertha Pratt Ehrmann. Desiderata. C1954.

www.ingramcontent.com/pod-product-compliance
Lightning Source LLC
Chambersburg PA
CBHW020913020526
44107CB00075B/1688